INTERVIEWOLOGY

INTER
VIEW
OLOGY

The New Science of Interviewing

ANNA PAPALIA

HARPER
BUSINESS

An Imprint of HarperCollins*Publishers*

In this book, I tell my story and the stories of my clients and students. In some instances, I have changed the names of my clients and students to protect their privacy. If I use a real name, I have gotten permission to do so. To outline the four interview styles, I have picked one client to represent each style; they are merely a representative and do not show a complete picture of that style.

HarperCollins books may be purchased for educational, business, or sales promotional use. For information, please email the Special Markets Department at SPsales@harpercollins.com.

FIRST EDITION

Library of Congress Cataloging-in-Publication Data
    Names: Papalia, Anna, author.
    Title: Interviewology : the new science of interviewing / Anna Papalia.
    Identifiers: LCCN 2023033136 (print) | LCCN 2023033137 (ebook) |
    ISBN 9780063327573 (hardcover) | ISBN 9780063327580 (ebook)
    Subjects: LCSH: Employment interviewing.
    Classification: LCC HF5549.5.I6 P37 2024 (print) | LCC HF5549.5.I6
    (ebook) | DDC 650.14/4—dc23/eng/20230830
    LC record available at https://lccn.loc.gov/2023033136
    LC ebook record available at https://lccn.loc.gov/2023033137

ISBN 978-0-06-332757-3

23 24 25 26 27 LBC 5 4 3 2 1

For my children, Simon and Eliot, my little Charmer and Challenger. Not only do I dedicate this book to you, but everything I do, I do for you.

For all the amazing people I've met and not met who are striving to interview better, this book is for you. In the words of my grandfather, "Today is the first day of the rest of your life."

Contents

Part III   Applying Interview Styles

How to Use This Book

I am assuming you're reading this book because you want to learn how to interview better. Congrats on taking the first step.

After doing loads of research and interviewing thousands of people, I discovered that we don't all interview the same way. Some people really relish the opportunity to answer questions about themselves. They love interviews. Others—those of you who just squirmed at the previous sentence—never feel comfortable in an interview, let alone get excited about them. Some people want to be liked, some want to be themselves, some need to get it right, and others just want to adapt. No approach is right or wrong, and there isn't one way to interview that's better than others.

But the interviewing advice that exists today doesn't take this into account. There are only two types of books on how to interview: books that are very, very specific based on your desired position or generalized books that offer boilerplate answers that you are supposed to memorize to land the job.

This book is neither of those.

This book is written for both job seekers and hiring managers and can be applied to any industry and any level. It will not provide you "perfect interview answers," because I do not believe there is such a thing. And I don't think "perfect interview answers" are what will land you the right job.

After a decade in HR and recruiting, and a decade as a career coach, I have extensive experience on both sides of the table, and I know one thing for sure: in the most basic sense, an interview is a set of questions about you, and if you know who you are and what you want, you will do better. It's the same for hiring managers. Knowing yourself, your biases, your preferences, and what impression you make helps you hire better. But none of the advice out there is geared toward figuring out who *you* are in an interview.

This book is.

Interviewology, the new science of interviewing, is based on my research and decades of experience. The foundation of interviewology is my discovery of the four interview styles—we don't all interview the same way, we interview in four distinct ways. You interview as either a Charmer, Challenger, Examiner, or Harmonizer. And here's the thing: all four interview styles are equally valuable. There isn't a style that is better or more effective.

In this book I share my research into these styles because I believe that having a deep understanding of how you and others interview can give you what you need to interview better. It's not scripted answers or trite advice but self-awareness. My hope is to provide a language to talk about our styles and revolutionize how we prepare for interviews.

In Part I, I share my story that led me to discover the four interview styles and why I think they are key to the future of interviewing. In Part II, I outline each interview style in depth: what they prioritize (for example, Charmers want to be liked, Challengers want to be themselves, Examiners want to get it right, and Harmonizers want to adapt); how to interview with each style; how to react to your opposite; strengths and overused strengths of each style; their different approaches; and what each style does to get people to see them as qualified. Finally, in Part III, I share what I've learned throughout my journey of discovering the four interview styles.

While there isn't one right way to interview, there are best practices that are more likely to make you successful. Do some people succeed by bucking convention and going against the norm? Absolutely, but it's rare. It typically helps to follow conventional wisdom. For example, getting to an interview fifteen minutes early is great advice across the board because it's harder to make a good impression after you've arrived late. Throughout the book I will share my best advice and tips on how to interview better for each interview style and in callouts called Interview Principles for Hiring Managers and Interview Principles for Job Seekers. I will also debunk some commonly held interview myths and reveal universal truths that I discovered in my research. These are also listed in the Appendix for easy reference.

In this book I share my personal story and the stories of my clients and students to inspire and encourage you to share your own story. My hope is that learning your style will help you discover the impression you really make in an interview so that you can learn to be the best version of yourself and not feel as though you have to pretend to be something you're not.

The Interviewology Profile

To help determine your interview style, I created a scientifically validated interview style assessment, which is a set of questions all about how you approach and perform in an interview. When you complete the assessment, you will be provided with an Interviewology Profile, a complete look at your results from the assessment. If you have already gotten an Interviewology Profile, you know that everyone's profile is different and yours outlines *you* in great detail—how *you* interview and what *you* need to work on. This book outlines all four styles more generally. If you haven't gotten an Interviewology Profile, I encourage you to do so. This book works in tandem with your Interviewology Profile. While you may be able to take a guess as to what your interview style is after reading this book, you may be surprised. Some introverts come across as extroverts in interviews. Some people who are Harmonizers at home are Charmers in an interview. Only way to know for sure is to take the assessment.

To discover your interview style and get an Interviewology Profile—a customized workbook on how you can prepare to interview—go to www.TheInterviewology.com/getmyprofile.

PART I

INTRODUCTION

1

An Interview Can Change Your Life

When I was fifteen, I moved out of my house to escape my abusive stepfather, who regularly beat me when he had a bad day . . . or for no reason at all. I knew I had to leave, but at fifteen I didn't have many options. Fortunately, my grandfather saved me and took me in. I found the only job I could: working at the sandwich counter in a gas station. My boss was understanding; she knew what I was going through, having herself left home at an early age. I felt lucky. I had a job, I had escaped my stepfather, and for the first time in more than seven years, I wasn't living in perpetual fear.

Then, a little over a year after living with my grandparents, I came home from school one day to find my beloved grandfather collapsed in the foyer. He had fallen down the stairs and crawled his way to the door but wasn't able to open it. He had been there for hours. The ambulance came and took him to the hospital, and we found out later that he had suffered a massive stroke. The damage to the right side of his brain was so severe that he would never walk or talk again.

I was devastated. The only person who had defended me and believed in me was gone. I was all alone again. My grandmother was preoccupied with her own grief and caring for him, ultimately becoming his full-time nurse.

One day, I came home from a long day of high school followed by a five-hour shift at the sandwich counter, and my aunt greeted me. She sat me down, a large black trash bag beside her. She clenched her jaw and wrung her hands. She'd come to help my grandmother and decided that the biggest help to her would be to clean house—and she was going to start with me.

She told me I had to go back and live with my mom and stepfather, but I refused. When she insisted, I told her I couldn't go back, that he beat me, and that I was scared. But she didn't listen, instead demanding my key to my grandparents' house. She wanted to make sure I knew I wasn't welcome there anymore. As I took the key from my pocket, I couldn't steady my hands enough to get the key off the key chain, so I just handed over the whole thing. It was an epoxy mold of a little seashell that my grandfather had given me years before on one of our beach walks. Without him and without that key, I was homeless.

I stood up, hefted that trash bag over my shoulders, and walked out. I was homeless for all of two blocks when I knocked on my boss's door with a tearstained face and she welcomed me in with open arms.

After a while, I got a better job at a bigger sandwich counter in a larger convenience store. My new boss owned the building, and there was an apartment above the store. When the previous tenants moved out, my boss offered it to me. A few of my coworkers became my roommates, and my boss took the rent out of my paycheck. Things were sorting themselves out.

Despite everything I had been through, I stayed in high school because my only goal was to go to college.

At the beginning of my senior year, I was struggling. Full-time school and full-time work was taking a toll, and I was petrified that I wasn't going to do well enough to graduate. I went to the principal and told her that I had moved out and I needed to work full-time to support myself but I still really wanted to go to college. I was worried that I wouldn't be able to go to school full-time and work enough to pay rent. She listened to me, nodded, and without saying a word walked me down the hallway to the guidance counselor's office. She instructed her to only sign me up for the classes that I needed to graduate. I only needed three classes, so that meant I only had to go to school from ten to one, giving me time to work.

I passed all three classes. I processed the grief. I worked. I paid rent. I graduated high school. The only thing that kept me going was the hope that I could get out of there. College was my way out. I lived in a small town, and everyone knew my story. College would give me a shot at blending in, at being normal and putting it all behind me.

I applied to the University of Pennsylvania to study psychology, and as part of the admissions process, I was asked to come in for an interview. I told them my story not because I was trying to pull on their heartstrings (because at the time I was *really* ashamed of it), but because I needed to explain why I didn't play sports and why my GPA and SAT scores were lower than their average applicant. I knew I wasn't like every other student who had applied, but I also knew that my experiences had given me something that my competition didn't have—determination and resourcefulness. I wanted them to know how hard I had worked and that I had done it all so I could get into college, which I saw as the ticket to changing my life.

At the end of the interview, the dean looked at me and said, "Well, Miss Papalia, you have a tough decision to make. You can wait for the letter, or I can accept you on the spot." I chose for him to accept me on the spot because I was pretty sure he would change his mind if I left.

My life changed in that interview.

The Second Interview That Changed My Life

I moved to Philadelphia and began studying psychology.

My freshman year in college, Stephen Starr, a now-famous restauranteur, opened his fifth restaurant on Penn's campus. He had a reputation for being tough to work for; jobs at his restaurants were hard to get, and servers were held to very high standards. Despite all of that, I wanted to work for him. His restaurants were popular, and I had heard rumors of servers making $500 in one shift. If I made that much money a few nights a week, I would be able to afford rent and tuition and it would give me time to go to class and study during the day.

The interview was a cattle call, and the competition was fierce. The interviews were held at the director of restaurants, Aimee Olexy's, desk in the middle of the open office. If there wasn't already enough pressure, all the waiting applicants were also watching. Aimee had a reputation for being quick and decisive. She only asked a few questions. I remember one: "What's your philosophy on waiting tables?" I said, "I believe in doing things right the first time. If you know a guest wants something a certain way, do it right the first time. Not just to make them happy but so you don't have to waste your time and do the same thing twice, because when it comes to busy restaurants, time is of the essence and guest satisfaction is paramount." As I was answering that question, I saw her eyes go from skeptical to pleased. It was the moment in an interview when you know you've got the job.

I worked for Stephen Starr for five years. I waited on celebrities, worked twelve-hour shifts, and stood up to bully chefs. I learned how to multitask. I learned how to sell. I learned how to talk to a room full of strangers. I learned how to be polished and professional.

I was drawn to hospitality because I am extroverted and I love people. Some people have an instinct for data, for nature, or for design. I always had an instinct for people. That's why I studied psychology. I wanted to figure people out.

In addition to my job at the restaurant, I also had behavioral health internships as a caseworker. I studied organizational psychology and abnormal psychology, created psychological experiments, and wrote lots of papers. But waiting tables wasn't just great money for me, it was also an extension of my psychology major. Every table was a new opportunity to figure people out. To try out a new tone of voice, a new approach, and a new way of interacting. I waited on thousands of people. I saw it as thousands of opportunities to change up my approach and receive real-time feedback. One big psychological experiment.

Being a server not only taught me how to adapt to everyone I worked with, but it taught me the importance of each individual hire. Each department in a restaurant has to work together to provide service, and when one department fails, everyone is impacted. That level of teamwork requires a thoughtful hiring practice, because when a bad hire happens, everyone in the restaurant feels it. In the cases where bad hires were made, I carefully brought it up to the general manager. One night, he threw his hands up and said, "If you think you can do a better job interviewing, you try it." So I did. I created interview liaisons from each department that would interview candidates. I figured we knew what it took to be successful, and if this person was going to work on our team, we should have a say in who got hired.

Waiting tables was a means to an end in college and I thought I wouldn't ever think about it again once I started my real career. But your first jobs stick with you. Working in restaurants is where I learned how to multitask, command a room, sell, and, most important, I became interested in the interview process. So I decided that working in the corporate world would be a better fit than becoming a psychologist. After five years I left to pursue a career in HR.

The Third Interview That Changed My Life

My first corporate job was in an eight-person human resources department for a large company as the HR generalist. My main responsibilities were keeping employee files up to date, conducting and proctoring pre-employment tests, and organizing a massive amount of paperwork. I got into HR because I had a knack for people, not paperwork, and I was quickly losing interest. Not to mention, I was actually bad at the job.

But then the corporate recruiter, who had too many jobs to fill, asked me to help her phone-screen candidates.

So happy not to have to do paperwork anymore, I jumped at the chance. I couldn't believe that they were going to pay me to talk on the phone and interview people all day. I loved it and was completely hooked. It's amazing the difference a job that taps into your natural skills can make. I was never formally trained for it, but as far as I could tell, neither was anyone else. I wasn't even told what jobs I was recruiting for; all I knew was that we had a lot of positions to fill and a lot of angry hiring managers who wanted candidates yesterday. No one ever gave me a manual or referred to one, and I learned years later it was because one didn't exist. We had positions to fill, and it was our job to fill them. That was our only guiding principle.

The more I interviewed people, the more I realized interviewing is a lot like therapy (perfect for a former psychology major): you ask candidates questions to try to find out what makes them tick and to see if they'd be a good fit for the role you're trying to fill. Your job is to figure out if people are lying to you or to themselves.

Like most hiring managers, I came to the job with my own personal biases and agendas. After years of working and going to school in high-pressure environments with high standards, professionalism and likeability were the most important characteristics for me when I was hiring someone. I disliked candidates who were not sophisticated and savvy. In all my years waiting tables, I honed the likeability and charm that I thought was required to get people to like me. And once in HR, I used those same metrics to determine if people interviewed well.

For me, interviewing was a performance, and likeability was the most important metric.

I was successful and good at interviewing, so I assumed if you didn't interview like me, or the way I thought you should, then you weren't prepared, you weren't a good fit, or you weren't qualified, and I would simply move on to the next candidate. At the time, I thought the only way to interview was the way I interviewed.

I left corporate HR a year later when I realized that I liked recruiting better, and I knew that if I wanted to become a great recruiter, I had to do it full-time while learning from other recruiters. So I went to work for a small boutique recruiting firm.

I learned, informally, how to recruit, how to cold-call, how to prepare candidates for interviews, and how to persevere. I learned that not all companies interview and hire the same way, and I learned the basic principles of interviewing. But probably the most important thing I learned was what successful candidates do, how they differentiate themselves, what they wear, how they act, how they answer questions, their attitude, their body language—the whole package. I learned what hiring managers liked, and I taught my clients how to do exactly that.

Contingency and retained recruiters work as an external arm of the recruiting function on an as-needed basis, so you fill a job and move on to the next opening. It can be frustrating as the circumstances change often: companies change their requirements, another recruiter fills the job you've been working on, or you recruit the perfect person, and the company makes them an offer, but the candidate turns it down. You control very little.

So, after two years, I left contingency recruiting to go in-house. I loved recruiting, but I missed partnering with hiring managers and being part of a team inside an organization.

I was recruited to work for an insurance brokerage that was previously part of a large bank, and I was the first hire after the company's divestiture. It was my job to hire for the new company that we were becoming. At the time, the company didn't have a name, a logo, or a culture, and I was tasked with helping figure out who we wanted to be and finding talent for that new identity. Being on the ground floor was entrepreneurial and very exciting.

I wrote position descriptions, advertised our jobs, and attended job fairs. I created internship positions, talent pipeline programs, employee referral bonuses, and a million other things. As a result, I was promoted in the first few months, and after a year and a half, I was responsible for the entire recruiting function and became *the* corporate gatekeeper. I partnered with every executive, created recruiting strategies for every position, and hired for every level of talent, from entry-level mail clerks to executive vice presidents. I felt like I was making a real difference.

I worked on gut instinct and made snap judgments. I decided who was worthy of a phone screen by scanning their resume for less than six seconds; internal referrals were highly favored. Anyone who had gaps in their employment, strange work histories, or typos on their resumes were immediately rejected. I was responsible for a lot of open positions at once, and the goal was to fill the roles as quickly as possible. My bonuses and evaluations were based on filling roles, not how I did it. So, for a decade, that's how I recruited. I was good at delivering what the hiring managers wanted, and because I was successful, I never questioned my methods. That came later.

After partnering with hundreds of hiring managers and interviewing thousands of applicants, I started to notice different hiring styles. Some hiring managers talked through the entire interview and never asked a candidate one question. Others depended on strange requirements and believed certain things made someone successful. I heard everything:

"They need to have played sports in college to be a good salesperson."

"I won't hire someone if they don't take notes in an interview."

"I won't interview anyone who doesn't have their GPA on their resume, and it has to be a 3.5 or better."

"GPA, what's a GPA? I just want someone who gets along with the team."

"They need to be likeable and fit in."

When your job depends on making hiring managers happy, you find them the athletes, the notetakers, the overachievers. You don't do it because you think those qualities are important; you do it because the hiring manager does. You do it because it's your job.

When you can't seem to find good people, managers assume it's because there aren't any good candidates out there. Recruiters and hiring managers tell story after story about how unprepared candidates are. It's always the candidate's fault. It's easy to blame your high turnover rate, hard-to-fill positions, and lack of good candidates on the talent pool. Rarely, if ever, is it attributed to a lack of leadership skills, a lack of training, or biased decision-making on the part of the managers.

When you are in a position of power, it's easy to blame the powerless.

In my last year as the director of talent, I started to look at candidates differently. In interviews, I started to see someone unprepared and faltering, and I wanted to help them, feed them the right answers, and coach them on how to negotiate. I am not sure how it happened or why my approach changed, but I remember the moment it did.

It was a day like so many before, full of back-to-back interviews, but on this day, one of them changed my life.

I was interviewing for an internal accounting position, and in all three interviews, I kept thinking, *We aren't clicking*. There was little rapport, I didn't feel as though I connected with any of the candidates, and I left the interviews wanting more. If this had happened in years past, I would've thrown out all three candidates and started over to find someone I clicked with. I don't know why, but I wondered if the candidates weren't the problem. I started to question my own motives and recruiting practices, and went back to my office to think.

I remember looking out my office window onto the man-made pond in the corporate complex and thinking, *Why do I need to click with this person?* I had never examined that thought before. I had never stopped long enough to ask myself *why* I preferred the candidates that I did. *Why am I looking for someone like me?*

Then I had a lightbulb moment that would change my perspective on hiring forever: *Am I biased?* That thought jolted me. *No. Me? Biased? No.*

This was long before diversity and inclusion training was as commonplace as it is today. I was perplexed and stared at the fountain in the middle of the pond. I thought about why I wanted to click with someone and why I felt that was a requirement. And I realized it was because that's how I interview. At that moment, I was humbled. I realized that for years the way I had been evaluating talent was all wrong, misguided.

One of my main criteria had been "clicking" in the interview, but I realized that clicking wasn't a job skill required for an accountant. This position was not client-facing, and they didn't have to build relationships. This role required general ledger accounting and reconciling accounts. When I set aside my own needs and saw the candidates for who they were, I realized what was truly required for the job, and "clicking" wasn't on the list. I looked back at the candidates I had interviewed with a fresh set of eyes, and there was one who was perfect for the job. But I hadn't been able to see it when I was judging him against what made *me* successful—an unfair measurement.

Then I thought, *How many candidates have I overlooked?* I continued to stare out onto the pond in disbelief and guilt. I made a promise to myself to do better.

I started examining all my thoughts around how we evaluated candidates and how I could help someone interview better. I became more focused on *how* we interview and how to improve the process for both job seekers and hiring managers.

No one was more shocked than me when I gave the president of the company my notice. I wanted to start my own business.

Key Takeaways

- An interview has the power to change your life.

- Most recruiters, HR professionals, and hiring managers are not trained to interview.

Coaching Tips

- Even though my story was unconventional, I learned a lot and gained incredible life lessons in the most unexpected places. The conventional path isn't the only path. What have you learned from your own path?

- What lessons did you learn in your early career that still influence you today?

- What are your biases in the interview process? What do you believe someone should do or say to come across as qualified?

2

How I Discovered the
Four Interview Styles

When I left my corporate job in the spring of 2011 to start consulting, I didn't have a business plan or a big client lined up. I didn't do it because there was a million dollars in it; I did it because I felt compelled to improve the interview process.

My first client was Temple University. I knew the dean because I had previously hired all of our interns from their prestigious risk management program. When he heard that I'd left the corporate world to consult, he asked me to redesign their professional development program and teach interview skills. In our first meeting he said, "Since you've been on both sides of the table, you know what they're doing right and what they're doing wrong."

I had to create the course from scratch. I wrote a handbook and curriculum on how to interview and designed a three-hour inter- active interview skills workshop. They gave me a stack of outdated handouts that they had been giving students since the 1980s. All those years recruiting on the corporate side gave me insight into what hiring managers wanted, but besides that, I didn't have much to go on.

I did some research and found that there simply weren't any tools to teach interview skills. There wasn't a textbook on how to interview. Most interview books only focus on one part: how to an- swer interview questions. I set out to write a comprehensive yet accessible how-to-interview handbook that would complement my course. What I came up with was a handbook with high-level tips, everything my students needed to know from what to wear, how to sit to look more confident, and the questions to prepare for.

For five years, I single-handedly supported more than six hun- dred students and two hundred private clients a year. I taught three three-hour interview skills classes a week. I conducted in-person twenty-minute resume reviews where I helped students edit, re- write, and format resumes. I conducted thirty-minute recorded mock interviews to give feedback on interview performance. In addition to working with the university, I consulted with large cor- porations on their recruiting operations and coached hundreds of hiring managers a year. It was like getting a PhD in interviewing.

I taught thousands of clients how to shake hands, how to craft a great elevator pitch, how to sit in an interview so they'd look less nervous. I rewrote thousands of resumes and sat with people as they cried, got angry, and stammered their way through a mock interview. I coached people on how to answer tough interview questions and how to negotiate, and I gave feedback from glowing praise to total disappointment.

I had clients from the most successful, polished executive vice presidents with thirty years in the corporate world, to college freshmen whose only work experience was a summer job scooping ice cream. They all came with different stories, but the theme was the same:

"I have had five interviews, and I keep getting passed over."

"I have an interview coming up, but I am terrified because I haven't interviewed in ten years, and the last time I did I bombed."

"Why do I get so nervous?"

"I am not comfortable talking about myself."

"I do not like interviews."

"I am bad at interviews. I will just never be good at them."

I had clients who were lost, insecure, defiant, scared, unsure, and worried, but they all had one thing in common: they wanted to interview better because they wanted to change their life by getting a new job or a promotion.

Some clients did the work, prepared, got better, and landed the job, but others just weren't getting it, and it wasn't because they didn't want a job. I just couldn't figure out why it wasn't clicking. I am sure every teacher at some point wrestles with those questions: Why aren't they getting it? Why aren't they doing their homework? Some of my students didn't even read the interview handbook that I had written.

In September 2016, we threw a big surprise fiftieth wedding anniversary party for my parents-in-law. Aunt Lynda flew out to the east coast for the party and we were sitting on the back porch on a perfect fall afternoon watching the koi fish eat in the pond of the backyard as we were catching up. Lynda is a great conversationalist; she is engaged and interesting and she asks the best questions because she has a childlike wonder, curiosity, and enthusiasm that is contagious. She was a teacher and she asked me how teaching at

Temple University was going. I shared with her what we were doing in my course, how great it was to be able to be the solution and help students and hiring managers learn how to interview after all the years of judging people on the other side of the table.

My style is not at all like Lynda's. I am direct and no-nonsense, and most are intimidated by me. I am enthusiastic, but I don't have the maternal warmth of Lynda. I confessed to her that I was having a hard time getting through to some of my students. No matter what I did, or how encouraging I was, some of them would still come unprepared for their resume reviews, bomb interviews, and not show up as their best selves at their internships. I took all of this personally. I didn't know why they weren't doing what they were supposed to.

Lynda, always thinking about others, proposed, "What if they have a different learning style? What if the way you're teaching them doesn't resonate with them?" Lynda went on, "When I was teaching, we were given training on learning and teaching styles, and it really helped me see others' needs and helped me better connect with my students. When I get back to San Francisco, I'll dig up the files I have and send them to you."

Lynda sent me the files, and it sparked something in me: I couldn't stop thinking about this difference. What if it was *how* I was teaching, not *what* I was teaching?

Learning styles is based on a theory by Howard Gardner, proposed in his 1983 book *Frames of Mind: The Theory of Multiple Intelligences*, in which he claims there are "eight types of intelligence: musical-rhythmic, visual-spatial, verbal-linguistic, logical-mathematical, bodily-kinesthetic, interpersonal, intrapersonal and naturalistic." Basically, this theory argues that who you are affects how you learn and how you should be taught. His philosophy was meant to empower learners and not limit them.

I thought about that for a long time and reflected, *Who are these students, who are they in interviews, who am I in an interview, and why does that change? How does it affect the type of advice I give them? Perhaps the way I do it isn't the way they would do it. Why are some of us different? And if we are different, that means I need to give students different advice.*

If it weren't for that conversation with Lynda, I am not sure I would've gone on to have my key insight into interview styles. Before knowing about the Multiple Intelligences Theory, I just gave advice from where I was, told people what to do based on what made me successful, but I didn't stop to consider if that advice would work for them. Lynda taught me that what makes me successful isn't necessarily what makes someone else successful. How I do it doesn't necessarily work for everyone.

At this point in my career, I had owned my business for six years. I'd consulted with companies and given them insights that changed their organization just by changing their interview process. I'd taught hiring managers how to interview better, and their departments improved. I'd taken the hire rate from 84 percent to 100 percent at Temple University's Fox School of Business risk management department. Students thanked me for helping them get internships; clients attributed getting their dream jobs to me. I had accomplished what I set out to do. I was using all the things I had learned on the other side of the table to help people. It was an extremely satisfying job, but I wasn't fully satisfied. I wanted to do more. I wanted to help more people.

In 2015, I had my first child. My priorities and the way I saw the world shifted. Having a child softened me, and as I saw people for who they were, I became more accepting.

When I was a recruiter, I made quick decisions based on the way someone interviewed. The quiet type, the salesy type . . . If they were too quiet, I assumed they were unprepared. Too talkative, and I figured they must be obnoxious. It wasn't deep. It wasn't considerate. In hindsight, I simplified and reduced complex decisions about people to trite shortcuts.

Then, when I became a coach, I had the opportunity to really get to know my clients. It was my job to ask them why they had a hard time opening up or why they approached the interview the way they did. I put aside my previous beliefs and listened. In doing so, I learned a lot from them.

They told me that they were uncomfortable telling their stories because they were private and didn't open up to anyone in the first five minutes, and I realized that it had nothing to do with how much they wanted the job or how qualified they were.

Others told me that they didn't want to prepare because they felt better when they winged it; that the preparation process made them feel too stale, too scripted. I realized that they wanted to feel a certain way in an interview, and that didn't mean their approach was wrong.

In our society, there is an assumption when teaching someone to interview that there is only one way to be. But it's also ambiguous—no one can put their finger on it; they just "know it when they see it." As a career coach, I heard this over and over again from clients who held themselves to an imaginary standard.

When I would coach hiring managers on evaluating candidates, they felt lost because they didn't know how to talk about candidates or the experience of meeting them. They believed the right candidate was supposed to act a certain way, and when they didn't, they were frustrated and felt like they were missing something. The way I did all those years ago.

As a coach, I now saw both hiring managers and job seekers struggling with the same thing equally. Everyone believing there was some standard but no one really knowing what that standard was.

I wanted to figure out a way to solve this problem. How do we make interviewing less ambiguous? How do we get around this idea that there is only one way to interview?

Then I had a lightbulb moment: What if there isn't just one way to be in an interview? What if, like the Multiple Intelligences Theory, there are *several* interview styles? What if the primary reason we get our wires crossed in an interview isn't because the person isn't qualified, but because we think we have the same criteria, but we don't? What if our beliefs about the way someone should be in an interview are different?

A More Scientific Approach

Given my background in psychology, recruiting, coaching, and teaching, I was in the perfect place to try to get to the bottom of this. I asked the university for permission to collect data and conduct research.

That spring, in 2017, I got pregnant with my second child. I also wrote the interview style assessment and tested it. I recruited friends, family, and old students to take it and give me feedback. Design is an iterative process, so during the day I wrote and adjusted and worked. I was pregnant with an idea and a baby, and both took up my every waking moment. I spent the summer getting bigger and bigger. I got up in the middle of the night and very early in the morning nauseated, and would steady myself by doing research on how people interviewed. What I discovered was a way to categorize how we interview. The interview style assessment proved my hypothesis that we interview differently and now I had data and a language to formalize how we talk about how we interview.

That fall, I introduced the interview style assessment as the first part of the nine-step professional development course I taught.

My students now had to take the ten-minute assessment to receive their Interviewology Profiles, which they would use as the course textbook. I trained my team of mock interviewers on the interview styles and had them write down what impression a student made in an interview, then we cross-referenced that with the results of the interview style assessment to verify that the self-reported data was correct. We found that the assessment was picking up on the same nuances that my mock interviewers were, and students were rating their profiles as very accurate. They started to see themselves in it and felt validated.

I named the assessment results the Interviewology Profile. I discovered that there wasn't one way to interview—there were actually four, which I named Charmer, Challenger, Examiner, and Harmonizer. This discovery led me to create a classification to diagnose someone's approach in an interview enabling us a common language to use and providing self awareness to my clients.

I tossed out the how-to-interview handbook that I wrote in 2011 and started using the students' customized Interviewology Profiles to teach them to interview. My students loved their Interviewology Profiles because they outlined what they needed to work on. They felt validated. I had one student tell me, "I didn't know other people interviewed like me. I thought I was the only one who did this." It also made my job as a coach easier because it gave me insight into their personality and what they needed to work on. It decreased the time I needed to get to know them in the coaching process, which allowed me to help them faster. It also gave me and my team of coaches great insight into ourselves and how we interviewed. I thought hiring managers could use the profile too.

Then, while I was consulting with a midsized firm to teach its female executives how to lead, I added the Interviewology Profile to the curriculum and tested it on hiring managers. Their Interviewology Profiles provided a classification, a way to organize hiring managers' preferences. Finally, I had the tool that I had wanted all those years before. A formalized language to use to think and talk about how someone interviewed.

I personally spoke with more than 180 clients after they received their results. I rewrote, synthesized, and added to the Interviewology Profiles based on their feedback. Personally, it challenged all my previously held beliefs, pushed me way out of my comfort zone, and taught me that I knew very little about interviewing all those years that I'd thought I was an expert. Doing that research was the culmination of all my skills and experience, years of making snap judgments as a recruiter, and years of getting to know my clients as a coach. It was fascinating, eye-opening, and compelling.

My daughter was born during a blizzard on a January night, and three days later I launched the Interviewology Profile website out into the world. Two births at once.

Now the interview style assessment was the very first step in my interview coaching process with all of our clients. I collected an evaluation from every person who took it and was obsessed with two metrics: Was it accurate, and was it helpful?

Every single person who took the assessment reported that their results were either "very accurate" or "extremely accurate." And my experience teaching it in person reflected that students understood themselves better, hiring managers found it illuminating, and my coaches could no longer imagine coaching without it.

After more than two thousand people took the interview style assessment, we had collected enough data to test its ability to meet the American Psychological Association for data reliability. I knew from my personal experience that clients found it to be accurate, but that was just anecdotal. The last step was to verify it using the highest standards possible. So in the spring of 2020, I hired the Assessment Standards Institute (ASI) to validate our interview style assessment. ASI is internationally recognized for their over forty years of experience evaluating data. They have extensive expertise in the understanding of assessment constructs and use of statistics to validate data reliability, construct validity, and disparate impact. I waited anxiously while they evaluated my data.

I was in the car, driving around aimlessly—because my son, now five years old, had fallen asleep while we were running errands and I wanted to let him nap—when my phone rang. It was ASI. I had been waiting for the call all week . . . Well, actually, I had been waiting for the call my entire career. I pulled over and held my breath. We made small talk and then Dr. Koerner and Dr. Watson congratulated me—we had met the APA standards for reliability. As of April 2020, three years almost to the day of writing it, my interview style assessment was scientifically tested and verified.

In 2023 after more than tripling our data set, I hired ASI again to test our data for data reliability, construct validity, and disparate impact. And again we met the standards and received a certified third-party evaluation. What is notable for my work and this book is that, though I knew there were four distinct interview styles, the Construct Validity assessment proves my hypothesis and therefore the thesis of Interviewology to be true. This lends credibility to the work and allows us to truly call this "the new science of interviewing."

What follows is the result of my research. For the remainder of the book, I'll dive into the four interview styles, backed by my scientifically validated interview style assessment, so that you can gain insight into the way you approach interviews.

Key Takeaways

- Interviewing better is not about *what* you are doing, but *how* you are doing it.

- When coaching and teaching, you first need to understand who your client is before giving advice or prescribing solutions, because what works for you doesn't work for everyone.

- The key to great interview prep isn't the right suit, it's self-awareness. In order to help more clients, I created an assessment tool that helps you gain self-awareness, a better understanding of how you really come across, and tips on how to improve it.

Coaching Tip

- Where have you been stuck, in the same way I was, where your approach no longer works? Where have you been insistent that your way is the right way even though it no longer serves you? Perhaps it's time to change up your approach, talk to someone who holds opposing views, and consider another way.

3

Why It's Important to Know Your Interview Style

Interviewing is by far the most common gateway to get an internship, job, or promotion, and it is expected to remain so, even with advances in technology- and AI-supported interviewing tools. For job seekers, your success at interviewing determines the opportunities that are available to you. For companies, interviews are equally significant; the most important business decisions are made in interviews. Who you hire changes your team, department, and the culture of your organization. The wrong hires can greatly impact the success of your team and the effectiveness of decision-making, and decrease your profit and return to shareholders.

Knowing your interview style helps you understand how you make an impression, how you get people to see you as qualified (or how you determine what makes someone else seem qualified), and what you prioritize in an interview.

The goal of interviewology is to start a new conversation about our unique approaches and give us a formalized language to talk about how we interview, because how weird is it that the most important business decisions are made in interviews, and yet we don't have a formal language to talk about someone's interview performance?

My goal is to move us from saying things like "I didn't like that candidate" in a debrief to saying, "I am a Harmonizer in interviews, and my wires get crossed with a candidate that starts off by asking me about sensitive subjects without building rapport first." Often, someone's interview style can get in the way of their being hired, and as hiring managers we need to take into account a candidate's interview style and how it interacts with our own. Perhaps asking tough questions is how they get someone to see them as qualified. Just because it's not the way you would interview, or it rubs you the wrong way, doesn't mean they wouldn't be great at the job.

Our first impressions are often wrong, and someone's performance in an interview is not always a good indicator of whether or not they can do the job. How many introverts do you know that love interviews? But that doesn't mean they can't be great at the job.

 INTERVIEW PRINCIPLE FOR HIRING MANAGERS

Our first impressions are often wrong, and someone's performance in an interview is not always a good indicator of whether or not they can do the job.

The Hiring Process Is Deeply Flawed

The stakes are high, but as you've seen in my story, we continue to get the interview process wrong—on both sides of the table. Like me, over 90 percent of the hiring managers I work with tell me that they were never trained to interview. As shown by researchers like David S. Pedulla in his book *Making the Cut*, a must-read about the current landscape in corporate hiring, there is no formalized way of interviewing, no accepted language or tools so it has been relegated to something hiring managers need to figure out on their own. In order to prepare for an interview, they Google it, wing it, or shadow someone. This produces unprepared hiring managers who make costly hiring decisions, which leaves a lot of room for bias. And job seekers aren't much better off, with most interview advice being written by the same people perpetrating such bias.

Our organizations do not represent our society's larger makeup. Females and African Americans are kept out of boardrooms and the C-suite. Diversity is a business incentive; organizations that are diverse perform better on all the metrics that shareholders care about, yet our biases keep diversity at a minimum.

It doesn't matter how committed an organization is or how much money it spends on diversity, equity, and inclusion training if they aren't training their hiring managers in how to interview with a more open mind. Because the only way an organization becomes more diverse is at the interview table. If the gatekeepers are handpicking people and positively reinforcing certain behaviors from a place of bias, they will create organizations that are skewed and populations that don't represent society but represent their biases.

INTERVIEW PRINCIPLE FOR HIRING MANAGERS

If the gatekeepers are handpicking people and positively rein-forcing certain behaviors from a place of bias, they will create organizations that are skewed and populations that don't repre-sent society but represent their biases.

For both job seekers and hiring managers, making complex deci-sions about people in a short interaction, like an interview, is hard. According to behavioral scientist Pragya Agarwal, "The brain is capable of processing approximately 11 million bits of information every second, but our conscious mind can handle only 40–50 of those bits. It is clear that much of our processing happens in our subconscious minds." To help us process all the rest of the infor-mation, our subconscious minds rely on shortcuts called heuristics, generalizations we make based on patterns we've observed. With so much to take in and so little time to do so, it makes sense that we fall back on heuristics to help.

But when it comes to looking for a job or hiring an employee, our heuristics get in our way. You've seen the articles a million times: "This CEO has the best interview question that will reveal if the applicant will be able to do the job"; "This CEO has *the* interview question that will reveal if someone will be a good hire." I am sure you have heard the urban legend of the hiring manager who takes a candidate to lunch and watches to see if you salt your food before you taste it, and deciding whether to hire you based on your choice. I've worked with CEOs and organizations that all have shortcuts like this or beliefs similar to my own insistence on "clicking" with candidates.

I met a CEO at a restaurant, and we were chatting while we were waiting for our table; after he learned what I did, he leaned into me and said, "Do you want to know *the one question* I ask all my candidates? If you were a crayon, what color would you be and why?" He puffed his chest up and expected me to praise him. Instead, I said, "Why would you ask that question? What does it have to do with the job you are hiring for? You are hiring for plumbers and electricians, right? So what does that tell you about their ability to do the job? Sure, I get it, you're trying to get to their personality, but there are much better ways to discover someone's personality than that." To say you have *the* question or *the* process means you are just hiring in a biased way. You're confirming the culture that you want to create. Hiring all the red crayons.

If you're a hiring manager and you think you have perfected it, you are either an amateur (you haven't been around long enough to have made great hiring mistakes), you are overconfident, or both. The way I was all those years ago as director of talent. I thought I had figured it all out but came to find out I was just hiring using my heuristics. It was quick, it was reliable, and it was effective . . . or so I thought. Knowing what I know now, I realize that I was hiring the same people over and over. I was trusting what I called my *instincts*, but now I know it was just implicit bias. Making snap judgments seems effective when you have thirty positions to fill, but I know now I was being closed-minded.

Why Our Privilege Matters

While my childhood was traumatic and my story is sad, my story and my life would be completely different if I were a person of color or if I had lived in North Philadelphia; Louisiana; inner-city Chicago; Appalachia, where the high school dropout rate is double the national average; or anywhere other than an upper-middle-class suburb in Maine that has one of the best high school graduation rates in the country. It was almost impossible to not graduate high school in Maine.

I can take a lot of credit for staying in high school and working hard, but here's the thing: my life was easy (in comparison). Although my grandfather suffered a stroke, leaving me alone at sixteen, the first sixteen years of my life I had him and my grandmother, who were both stable, mentally healthy, college educated, and upper-middle-class. I can't take all that for granted.

My story and who I am would be different if I hadn't had all that privilege. I was surrounded by support systems, and I was raised in a family where everyone was college educated. I never thought that college was out of my reach, or a good education would be unattainable. What if I had been a first-generation student, trying to navigate college applications and financial forms in a second language? I knew how to apply to an Ivy League school because I had seen so many people do it. I was more a result of my environment and generational wealth than my own ability to "pull myself up by my bootstraps."

It would be shortsighted, unfair, and uneducated for me to say that I am who I am because I am brave and conquered the odds. To be honest, the odds where in my favor as a white woman. When I think about my journey in this context, I understand just how much invisible help I had. Would I have gotten into Penn if I hadn't looked the way I do? Would I even have thought to apply to Penn if I hadn't grown up where I grew up?

There are people in the world that are discriminated against for so many reasons, even something as simple as the name on their resume. For example, in a large study, researchers sent an identical resume to companies in Boston and Chicago, changing only the candidates' names. On some resumes they put traditionally African American–sounding names like Tamika, Aisha, Rasheed, and Tyrone, and on others Caucasian-sounding names, like Brendan, Greg, Emily, and Anne. They found that it takes fifteen applications for an African American to get one call back, whereas it takes a Caucasian ten applications, proving the implicit bias in recruiting and hiring. It's not for people like me that I feel drawn to improve the interview process; it's for those that are shut out and left behind. Those who don't have the opportunities and help that I did.

Hiring well means understanding that the process is flawed with implicit bias and systemic racism. That the system only works for some. It means understanding that unpaid internships aren't equal opportunities because only the elite can afford to work for free. So judging a resume based solely on work experience is not fair because our experiences of work are not equal. Some, like me, had to work their way through college. Others had parents who paid for school, so they could afford to take low-paying internships or study abroad for a semester. The system that we use to determine talent doesn't take any of this into account.

The disparities in opportunities and salaries don't stop there. Wage inequality, promotional opportunities—the list goes on. Not to mention people who are trying to get a job after being incarcerated—the likelihood of someone getting and keeping a job after serving time is 33 percent. As a society we do a terrible job of ensuring that everyone has a shot.

Representation matters and diversity is important because it is the right thing to do. Diversity is simply creating organizations that reflect our society. And the way to create a diverse company is to train hiring managers how to be more open-minded because the interview table is where we decide who to hire and thus how diverse our company is.

To be better recruiters, better hiring managers, better bosses, we must take all of this into account. That the majority of HR professionals are white women and the majority of executives are white men, and where they come from is not where everyone else comes from. And even if your life was hard, like mine, most of us are enormously privileged. We won't change anything about the interview process until we acknowledge this.

The Power of Self-Awareness

Self-awareness is when your words and actions are in alignment. In psychology this is called congruence, when your self ratings are consistent with your actions.

I believe self-awareness is the most critical component to a great interview. It is the key to acknowledging and dismantling the pervasive bias that leaves us all at a disadvantage. It is also the key for job seekers to improve their interview performance. It should be your guiding principle whether you're a job seeker, college student, hiring manager, or company. Self-awareness isn't easy—some studies report that only 10 to 15 percent of people are truly self-aware—but that's the magic of the four interview styles and the Interviewology Profile. Knowing your interview style is a door to a much deeper self-awareness.

Just as we don't all interview the same way, we don't all have the same story and we certainly have not all come from the same place with the same opportunities. Building our self-awareness, whether through learning our interview style, or reflecting clearly on our personal story or bias, allows us to not only interview better, but also to make better decisions about what we want.

According to organizational psychologist Tasha Eurich, "Research suggests that when we see ourselves clearly, we are more confident and more creative. We make sounder decisions, build stronger relationships, and communicate more effectively . . . We are better workers who get more promotions. And we're more-effective leaders with more-satisfied employees and more-profitable companies." There is a power in self-awareness.

For Job Seekers

Conventional interviewing advice is often reduced to getting there on time and reciting perfect answers to tough questions. But I never saw it that way. I noticed my clients' problem was lacking self-awareness, not failing to memorize the perfect answer. It wasn't a script they needed, it was a mirror, insight into the impression they were making. They needed help understanding who they were.

We all have an idea of how we come across, and when we are in an interview, we become hyperfocused on the impression that we make. *Did I come across the way I intended to? Did they think I meant something else? I hope they didn't misunderstand.*

We all have a need to be heard and understood, but the dynamics of traditional interviews make that more difficult. When there is something on the line as important as a job, it makes you second-guess yourself. If you are unprepared or don't know yourself very well, you often feel lost. Knowing yourself is like a guiding light, because no matter how strange, how difficult, or how intimidating the interview, you can rely on your self-knowledge. You don't have to memorize the perfect interview answers; you don't have to rely on what you think you are supposed to say. Instead, you are confident because it comes from the most authentic place—*you*.

To better understand who you are is hard. The good news is that if you are looking for a job, all the things you need to do, like update your resume, practice interview questions, and research what you want in your next role are all great exercises to build up your self-awareness. Thinking about how to brand yourself, putting yourself out there, and asking for recommendations and referrals, is a great practice in being vulnerable. In a job search you have to endure a lot of uncertainty. It's a wonderful time to get some clarity on who you are and what you want. Self-awareness is often divided into two types, internal and external, and interviewing pushes on both. Internally, you reckon with the feelings and thoughts you have about yourself and your career. With external self-awareness, you have to become more attuned to the impression you make and how it aligns with your intention. Knowing your interview style helps with this. It will clearly reveal what you prioritize in an interview so you can better prepare, leverage your strengths, and sell yourself. It'll also teach you about the other styles so you can shift your approach to accommodate the person interviewing you.

For College Students

One of the hardest aspects of interviewing as a college student is that there is already an enormous pressure to fit in and go with the flow. An interview demands that you tell me who *you* are, not who your friends are or how you identify in regard to a group or your class or your major. Interview prep is the time for you to wrestle with decisions you've made and get clarity on why *you* did what you did, how you got to where you are, and why you want to go where you want to go. You can't answer these questions if you are thinking about yourself as part of a larger group, or worse, worried about what your sorority sisters would say.

Self-awareness will help you answer questions like *Can you tell me why you majored in what you majored in? Can you tell me why you want to work in this industry?* not with boilerplate answers but with a deeper and more thoughtful response.

Knowing your interview style can also give you confidence when you lack professional experience. Armed with the knowledge of who you are, you can make a more authentic impression. Presenting yourself with pride and confidence puts you at the top of interview lists. Often college students doubt they have anything to offer and wonder why they should be hired, falling into the mental trap of not knowing who they should be and how to present themselves.

Knowing your interview style will give you a foundation that allows you to be yourself, not pretend to be anything other than that.

For Hiring Managers

I know you think you can interview by just "having a conversation" with candidates because you "just want to get to know them." And I know that you are very busy and the last thing you have time for is creating an interview protocol; you just need to hire someone. But bear with me for a moment: If you do that—just hire someone—you aren't solving the problem, you are creating a bigger problem. With this approach, you're more likely to hire the wrong person, costing you way more in time and money than if you had just created a good interview protocol from the beginning. Estimates are that poor hires can cost upward of $17,000 to $224,000 per person in lost productivity and training hours; it's not worth being unprepared.

Just hiring anyone is not what you want; you want to hire the *right* person, and there is a scientific way to do that. We know that ambiguity leads to bias. The more structured your interviews, the better and more diverse your hires can be. You must prepare appropriate interview questions that relate to the job—before the interview—and ask every candidate the same questions.

There is a lot of research that says we are easily swayed by beauty; the halo effect, the tendency to make a judgment on someone based on our feeling about one singular quality; and the "like me effect," the tendency to like those who are similar to ourselves. If you want to prevent yourself from making biased decisions, start with learning your interview style. That will show you what priorities you have and what you prioritize in candidates. It will reveal how your approach affects the way you judge others. You can also write down what you want out of a candidate ahead of time, so you don't find yourself swayed by first impressions, and recruit an accountability partner to hold you to it. This is key because for hiring managers, the biggest impediment to self-awareness is their power. Studies show that senior leaders and people with power have blind spots because they lack a group of peers that hold them accountable. That's because the more power you have, the less likely people are to critique you. So find people you trust to hold you accountable.

You should also practice before the interview. The more you interview, the better you get, and this is true for hiring mangers as well. The average job seeker looks for a job for six to nine months and may go to as many as thirty interviews. If you are a manager with low turnover, you may interview twice a year. That means that candidate has more experience at the interview table than you. You need to understand this and acknowledge how it affects the interviews you give. While, yes, it's true that you have the "power" in the interview, it's sort of like a driver's ed instructor being driven around by a fifteen-year-old. Sure, you have the power, and you are in the driver's seat, but that doesn't mean you know what you are doing.

You need to adequately prepare for interviews and have a procedure and plan that you practice and execute. Don't assume that just because you know the job you will be a good interviewer. The best technical experts I know are not great interviewers. And don't start thinking that just because you have the power that means you must be good at it. You get good at it by practicing, making a bunch of bad hires and figuring it out. There's no other way. If you think you have perfected this, you are doing it wrong.

For Companies

Companies are just groups of people. Groups of people have values and ideas and want to keep those values and ideas safe from other groups of people. Just like people, companies can lack self-awareness. External self-awareness for companies is how a company looks from the outside. Internal self-awareness is how it feels when you work there.

Too often, the picture that companies paint of themselves doesn't align with the experience of working within the organization. It can come from a good place with strong missions, values, and goals, but if these were created by executives too far removed from the day-to-day, they can feel more like corporate mandates than a reflection on the true spirit of the organization. A disconnect.

How does an organization check its self-awareness? You can start by collecting data. Research shows that in order to get someone to act, you must show them data that proves how they are part of the problem. Test all your hiring managers' interview styles and collect data to see if they are hiring the same person over and over.

You can also create flatter organizations to limit each individual's power, because not only is power not good for their personal self-awareness, it also affects the company's self-awareness.

Empower everyone through accountability and decrease big decisions being made in a vacuum, especially interviews. Create interview teams made up of diverse hiring managers who have to come to a consensus. Create a culture where diversity matters and procedures enhance that diversity.

Much like a self-aware person, a self-aware company attracts employees because it knows who it is; it's not perfect and doesn't pretend to be; it tries hard to do the right thing but embraces failure. People want to work at places where they can be human, and we want to feel like our companies are run by humans.

The Science Behind the Test

It was very important to me that the interview style assessment be scientifically sound; we are proud that we have a normal distribution in our data, validated by the Construct Validity test performed by ASI, meaning there is no gender, racial, or age bias to interview styles.

The overall goal of the interview style assessment is to educate people on the assumptions they make based on someone's interview style. It is a tool backed by science and data to provide insight and to decrease the amount of guesswork, mind reading, and ambiguity in the hiring process. Reducing ambiguity also reduces biased decision-making, which typically relies on gut instincts, following the pack, or leaning on old behaviors. Other than leading to bias, these approaches don't reliably result in getting the right job or hiring the right person.

There has been no system, no language or accepted interview protocol, until now. Is knowing your interview style the entire solution to our flawed hiring processes? No. But it is part of the solution. The other part is standardizing the interview process, creating systems that decrease bias, and educating on how the way we were doing things affects productivity and ultimately success.

In my organization we don't just train hiring managers how to interview, we also show them data. We assess hiring managers' interview style, and it gives us an overview of their cultural makeup. Then we ask if their data reflects the broader population or if it is skewed.

What we know about diversity, equity, and inclusion training is that the only training that is successful is the one that provides data. We need to see how our decisions affect the broader culture. We need to see ourselves as part of the problem before we act or change.

In an interview on PBS, Anthony Greenwald, the father of the implicit bias test, which revealed that implicit bias shows up in 70 to 75 percent of Americans, pointed to a lack in scientific testing as the key failure with existing diversity and implicit bias trainings. Without data, he said, trainings "can be deployed without actually achieving anything." You cannot solve a problem without truly knowing the problem, and data is the most accurate way to define a problem.

With the interview styles, we can use data to examine bias in an organization. For example, data gathered from everyone who has taken the interview style assessment shows that there is a proportionate distribution among the styles. Which means that a non-biased organization should reflect that. Organizations should all look like Figure 1:

FIGURE 1
Distribution of interview styles among the general population.

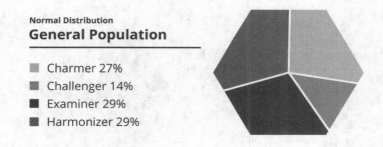

Normal Distribution
General Population

- Charmer 27%
- Challenger 14%
- Examiner 29%
- Harmonizer 29%

Instead, most companies aren't so equally distributed; they tend to prefer one or two styles based on the individuals who work there and, specifically, those who conduct the hiring. Figure 2 shows two examples from companies that I have worked with.

As you can see in Figure 2, companies are typically biased toward one or two interview styles over others. We can use this interview style data to have a conversation about preferences. It can reveal the true feelings and desires of hiring managers. If your organization skews toward Challengers, as with Company A, your hiring managers are looking to hire more Challengers and may dismiss candidates with other styles. Personality assessments, like the interview style assessment, reveal our biases; they don't create them.

We can use this data to train our hiring managers to interview better by seeing that the decisions they make at the interview table have a great impact on the company. We need a system that keeps our hiring managers educated and accountable. Currently

FIGURE 2
Distribution in Company A versus Company B

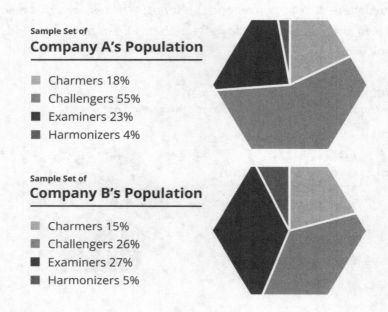

Sample Set of
Company A's Population

- Charmers 18%
- Challengers 55%
- Examiners 23%
- Harmonizers 4%

Sample Set of
Company B's Population

- Charmers 15%
- Challengers 26%
- Examiners 27%
- Harmonizers 5%

recruiters are not held accountable for how they treat applicants, and the requirements they use to determine who gets passed on to the next round are often opaque and vague. Applicant tracking systems are rife with bias and prevent 75 percent of resumes from ever being seen by a human. The interview style assessment can provide the data we need to solve these problems.

Key Takeaways

- The most important business decisions are made in interviews. Who you hire changes your team, the effectiveness of the department, and the culture of your organization, yet 90 percent of hiring managers are never trained to interview.

- The interview process, as it currently stands, is deeply flawed. A lack of training among hiring managers, standardized procedures, and data has led to pervasive bias.

- No matter what new technology is trendy, nothing, no artificial intelligence, can tell YOUR story. Nothing can replace knowing yourself and practicing to interview better.

- Your interview style provides key insight that can improve your self-awareness, making you a better interviewer no matter what side of the table you are on.

Coaching Tips

- Reconsider the story you tell yourself by thinking about it differently the way I did mine. What invisible help did you have that you have never thought about? In what ways have you taken personal responsibility for your "success" or "story," but in reality the odds were in your favor? Reimagine yourself with less in order to see how much you really have.

- Having keen self-awareness and being authentic is not about being unfiltered; it's not saying whatever comes to mind. It's about integrity; staying true to yourself doesn't mean voicing every opinion, just the ones that matter to you. Do you know what matters to you?

- Interviews are often very casual and unscientific, which leads to bias. Where have you resisted making the interview conversation structured and why?

- In terms of your self-awareness, what are you pretending not to know? Do your words line up with your actions? Are your inner and outer selves in alignment? In what ways are you being perceived that you're not aware of?

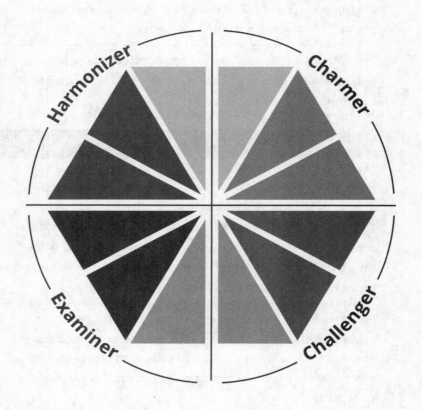

4

The Four Interview Styles

Everyone has a different approach to job interviews, and unfortunately, people don't always represent themselves well. Some people downplay their strengths, some people lie, and others turn on the charm. The differences have nothing to do with their work history, their race, or their lack of morals—they have everything to do with their unique interview style.

Through my research, I discovered that there are four primary interview styles that people fall into. These can be most easily defined by their priorities in an interview.

- *Charmers think,* I want to be liked.
- *Challengers think,* I want to be me.
- *Examiners think,* I want to get it right.
- *Harmonizers think,* I want to adapt.

And, contrary to what many books or websites about interviewing say, there isn't any one right way to interview. What's more important is understanding who you are and how to present yourself in the most clear, confident, and authentic way.

For example, not everyone goes into an interview wanting to be liked. While on some level we all want to be liked, when it comes to interviews, making a good impression is more important than being liked. Each style's approach to making a good impression is unique:

- *Charmers show their value by being eager.*
- *Challengers show their value by questioning.*
- *Examiners show their value by being precise.*
- *Harmonizers show their value by being agreeable.*

And this sets each style up for different experiences. Your interview style outlines not only who you are in an interview and how you come across, but also how you see interviews and what the experience is like for you.

- *Charmers see an interview as a performance—it's a stage and they are the star of the show.*
- *Challengers see an interview as a cross-examination, and they need to get their questions answered.*
- *Examiners see an interview as a test that will be graded as pass or fail.*
- *Harmonizers see an interview as a tryout for a team that they want to join.*

Within these four primary styles, I've found that there are twelve variations caused by overlap between the styles. For example, if you are a Charmer, you can have tendencies of a Harmonizer or a Challenger, and these tendencies also affect the way that you approach an interview. In Part II, we'll dive more deeply into each style, what they are, how to determine which style is yours, and the different variations within each. At the end of each style chapter you'll find the breakdown of the two variations of each interview style.

Your interview style doesn't change depending on how prepared you are for an interview; it isn't prescribed because of the type of job you have or your race or your gender—not all engineers interview the same way, just as not all African Americans interview the same way (and we have the data to prove it). Your interview style is like your personality. It is stable and predictable. But your personality is not set in stone either; it's what you decide to do with the traits you are given. You can't choose your interview style, the same way you can't choose your personality, but you can shift your style to draw upon your strengths and perform better. Your interview style is your natural tendency; it is not your destiny. We all have all the styles within us, and when we know our baseline, or the style that we tend toward, we then can shift more authentically.

How Your Interview Style Is Measured

Though we often think of behavior in binary terms (quiet or loud, leader or follower), it's more accurate to think of it as a spectrum. No one is ever 100 percent one way or another. With this in mind, the interview styles are measured on two scales: introversion to extroversion and steadfast to accommodating. See where you fall on these scales in your Interviewology Profile.

There are a few characteristics of each of these that help to determine where on the scale you land.

INTROVERTS

- *Introverts are energized by alone time.*
- *Introverts do not open up right away and prefer to keep things to themselves.*
- *An interview is not a natural setting for an introvert.*
- *Introverts think to speak, so talking and thinking on their feet doesn't come naturally.*

EXTROVERTS

- *Extroverts are energized by other people.*
- *Extroverts open up easily and share details about themselves.*
- *An interview is a natural setting for an extrovert.*
- *Extroverts speak to think, so talking and thinking on their feet comes naturally.*

STEADFAST

- *Internally focused. Taking cues on how to answer from themselves.*
- *Neither a positive nor negative response from the interviewer elicits a change in their style.*
- *Prefer to be consistent; unwavering commitment to the facts. No matter the audience.*

ACCOMMODATING

- *Externally focused. Taking cues on how to behave and respond from others.*

- *Change easily depending on the verbal and nonverbal feedback they receive from others.*

- *Prefer to adapt to the room, audience, and energy they perceive.*

How closely you identify with each of these statements determines how close to each side of the spectrum you are. It's important to remember that none of us is totally introverted or extroverted, just as no one is totally steadfast or accommodating. Circumstances and situations, and organizational and power dynamics, change how we behave.

Your interview style gives you a sense of where you generally fall on each scale, and knowing where you fall on the scale allows you to manage your expectations around how much you can shift your behavior.

The Interview Effect

It's important to note that the interview style assessment specifically assesses how you are in an interview, not necessarily how you are in other settings, which differentiates it from more generic personality tests. Many personality factors are consistent across different situations, such as introversion versus extroversion: if you're extroverted in real life, you're likely to be the same in an interview. Interestingly, though, sometimes people change in interviews: introverts occasionally open up, while some extroverts unexpectedly clam up.

As a recruiter, I saw this play out many times. It was that thing we couldn't quite put our finger on that we subsequently dubbed the Interview Effect. I would interview someone who presented as bold and talkative, but the moment I hired them, they turned into a different person, or vice versa.

I discovered that most hiring managers usually assume that people are the same all the time, so how they interview must be how they are in a work setting. When that turns out not to be the case, hiring managers often feel duped, and employees find themselves in the wrong positions.

I had a student, Ryan, whom I had known for three years, take the assessment. He had a reputation for being a guy who couldn't stop talking once he started. If he caught you in the hallway, he'd walk with you wherever you were headed to keep the conversation going. One day after class, he walked with me all the way to my car. He talked to *everyone*, yet his Interviewology Profile results came back as introverted. When I met with him to discuss it, he said, "Oh yeah, totally. I shut right down in an interview. I just wait and listen. It's really hard for me to talk the way I normally do. It's something about the interview. It changes me."

So while I had a hunch that an interview was not the best indicator of personality, now I had some scientific proof: interviews change people.

An interview is an artificial event where someone has something you want, a job or a promotion, and you need to act a certain way to get it. And that "certain way" is different for everyone. For Ryan, an open and talkative person, he had absorbed some story from society or his family that he couldn't be himself in interviews, that he was not "supposed" to be talkative in that setting, that he had to wait his turn and tell them what they wanted to hear.

All Styles Are Valuable

Here are two things I know to be true after coaching thousands of clients: Everyone gets better at interviewing; the more you do it, the better you get. I have never seen anyone get worse. And everyone is capable of interviewing better; no one is without room for growth.

When I embarked on this research, I hypothesized that there would be one interview style that was more successful. Year after year I saw students and clients nail interviews, and I assumed we would discover the right way to interview.

But what I learned changed everything.

I looked back at years of interview notes and data on which students got the most internship offers and how that correlated to their interview styles, and there wasn't a clear winner. Every style was represented. Our most successful students, the ones who got the most internship offers, the most full-time job offers after graduation, and those who felt most confident in interviews were represented by all four interview styles.

As I've already stated, an interview is just a set of questions about yourself, and those who know themselves well are more likely to do better in interviews. This self-awareness is the indicator of success, not your interview style.

And there isn't one style that naturally has more self-awareness. There isn't one style that is better or more successful in interviews as either hiring managers or job seekers. There isn't one style that has a leg up or a natural advantage—those beliefs I'd held were my biases. I learned that we all assume our style is the best. Our biases are born in our preferences.

We all prefer to interview with others who share our interview style. Like me all those years ago not wanting to hire an accountant that I didn't "click with." We are the most comfortable and most secure when we interview someone who "speaks our language," but our preferences are one of the biggest obstacles that get in our way. We can overlook great people.

Knowing your style can explain your bias, and an understanding of all four styles will help you interview better with everyone, not just those who have the same style as you.

How the Interview Assessment Compares to Other Personality Assessments

Though we focus strictly on how people perform in job interviews, clients tell us that their Interviewology Profile results often line up with those from other personality assessments, such as DISC, Myers-Briggs, and StrengthsFinder, to name a few. We like that clients feel they get similar results because it provides another level of validation for them, giving them further confidence in our assessment.

But because our test focuses on how you are in an interview, it could potentially change over time, unlike a Myers-Briggs, which is NOT based in science and operates under the assumption that your personality is fixed over the course of your life. We assess what you believe and how you behave *today*, which means that as you gain more interviewing experience, your results may change to reflect your new skills. The Interviewology Profile is perceptive enough to pick up on nuances and variations as you evolve.

This was true for one of my students, Priya, who took the interview style assessment as a freshman and learned she was an Examiner, which she felt was accurate. But when she returned as a sophomore and took it a second time, her results indicated she was a Charmer (the polar opposite style), so I asked her to see me after class, worried it was a mistake.

When I asked her about the change, she confided in me that

though she had been an Examiner, interview experience and an internship had shown her how she wanted to act in professional settings. So her behavior had changed and so had her interview style. I was relieved and happy that she didn't feel boxed into a particular style and that our results accurately reflected her growth.

What's more, none of us are just one interview style; everyone is a blend of all four, and you prioritize your primary style. In practical terms, this means that sometimes you may be more of a Challenger than a Harmonizer because different people bring out different facets of your personality. And knowing your interview style will give you insight into your natural tendencies so that when you shift between these various facets, you do so authentically. I have learned that when you see yourself clearly, you know how to sell yourself well by appreciating your unique talents and what you can bring to the table.

My Intention and Goals

I am sure there will be skeptics who might say that putting people into categories is the opposite of appreciating someone's uniqueness. But the depth and detail that go into the assessment are based on the fundamental principle that giving people information so they can better understand themselves is helpful. These categories are not meant to minimize differences or create systems that are biased against certain types. Rather, my decades of interviewing experience have taught me that while we are all different, there are certain overarching behaviors that make us more alike than we might realize. And when people see themselves reflected in videos or stories, they often feel reassured. That reflection and understanding provides a sense of place, security, and validation.

Humans have always searched for ways to help them better understand themselves. For a long time, it was through archetypes, stories, and folklore. Today we are more likely to consult Google, TikTok, YouTube, self-help books, and personality assessments, but the goal is the same: to feel seen and validated.

In my experience, my clients see themselves in their Interviewology Profiles and they know it's not meant to reflect the entirety of who they are. Everyone I work with (even the critics) finds which aspects resonate with them and which don't and then takes what works for them. I am not in the business of telling people who they are; I am in the business of holding up a mirror to empower them. I want my clients to be more confident, which doesn't come from pretending to be something you're not or memorizing answers. The confidence that gets you hired comes from self-awareness—knowing who you are and being fully aligned with it.

I teach my clients that their true value comes from their whole lived experience, not just their resume qualifications. I teach them to think about what their unique value propositions are and how to build a personal brand based on their individual strengths. To do this, they must first have a strong grasp of their basic personality and the impression they make. Taking the assessment and finding out their interview style helps crystallize this for them.

One of the most common desires people have is to find out what others think of them. In research done by psychologists Nicholas Epley and Mary Steffel, in which they asked five hundred Americans to imagine that they had a "brainscope" that would allow them to see into other people's minds and know what others were feeling and thinking with total accuracy, researchers were surprised to learn that most people didn't want to peer into the minds of the rich, famous, and powerful. Instead, the vast majority wanted to know what those they knew best thought of them. They wanted a magical mirror they could hold up to themselves. The interview style assessment is like that mirror—it gives you the insight that so many job seekers and hiring managers crave.

The assessment doesn't prescribe an identity. It is my sincere hope that the interview style assessment gives you this glimpse into how others see you. It is simply a tool to help you estimate how you come across in an interview. It's up to you to use this knowledge to improve—whether you're a hiring manager using this insight to open up to different candidates or a job seeker cutting back on your overused strengths to perform better. We'll get into how to make those changes in Part II.

Key Takeaways

- Your interview style is based on how you would typically interact in an interview situation. This is not necessarily how you act all the time.

- Your interview style is simply a snapshot in time. Your assessment results determine where you are today, but you will learn how to shift as you gain more interviewing experience. Your interview style may change as you grow and evolve and may carry different meaning to you over the years. You may become more comfortable opening up and learning how to talk about yourself; you may also learn how to ask great questions, or how to feel more comfortable in an interview setting. Your interview style may change, but over 88 percent of clients get the same results year after year.

- You are a blend of all four interviewing styles, but your primary style is the product of the skills that you prioritize. One style isn't better or more ideal than the others—they are equally important and valuable.

- Interviewing well is an act of adapting to another person and flexing your style. Your interview style is the same whether you're a job seeker or a hiring manager. The interview style assessment determines how you react in an interview regardless of which side of the table you are on.

Coaching Tips

- What are some of the stories and messages that you have internalized that tell you that you can't be yourself in an interview? Do you think you have to be a certain way in order to get someone to hire or admit you?

- What does the "interview effect" do to you? Does an interview change you? Are you naturally quiet but become more open in interviews? How can you align more of who you are naturally with who you show up to be in an interview?

PART II

WHAT'S YOUR INTERVIEW STYLE?

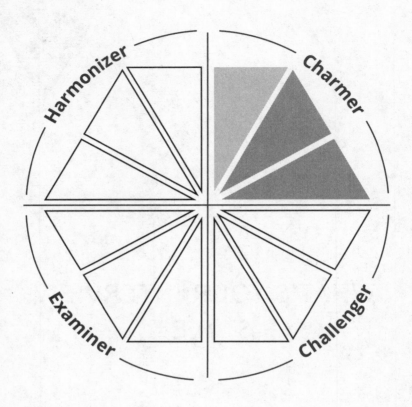

CHARMER. They are engaging in interviews. They are externally focused and easily open up in interviews and seek approval of the interviewer. They make the interviewer feel like they are interested in every word they say. They can easily speak about themselves and their work experience. Their keen ability to figure out where the conversation is going helps them give quality answers and make a good impression. This style is about being prepared on all fronts so that they can leverage their pre-interview practice and research to make a connection with the interviewer. Making a good impression is very important to Charmers.

5

Charmer

"I want to be liked."

It shouldn't surprise you that I love interviews. I've spent my career interviewing and teaching interview skills. When I got my start in recruiting and HR, I assumed that everyone loved to interview like me. Of course, I knew that people would get nervous for an interview, but I believed everyone approached interviews the same way I did—excited about the opportunity to sell themselves and really energized by the process.

That's because I am a Charmer, and Charmers love to interview.

When I discovered and started researching the four interview styles, I was sure that I would find that Charmers were the best at interviewing. Mainly because Charmers love to interview, and let's be honest, I am biased. But after years of teaching interview skills and researching interview styles I realized I was wrong.

Well, I was wrong about one part. Charmers like to interview more than the other styles, that's true, but they aren't *better* at interviewing than the other styles.

With this realization, I stumbled upon a universal truth, which is that we all have a tendency to think that everyone interviews the way we do. We also think that our way is the best way. Of all the people whom I have studied, they have all said that their interview style is the best style—even those who know they can improve feel that their general approach to interviewing is the right way.

So, while Charmers aren't any better at interviewing, in our society we have a bias toward extroversion and being accommodating in an interview, two things Charmers do well. After I discovered the interview styles, I saw this bias clear as day. Extroverted candidates are hired more frequently not because they are more qualified but because they interview "better," according to our society. If you're a hiring manager, please reread that sentence. Are you contributing to this bias with your hiring practices? My hope is that by having a clear understanding of Charmers' style, we can move past this bias and hire with a more inclusive mindset.

Charmers See Interviews as a Performance

Most people don't enjoy opening up and answering questions about themselves, especially after only five minutes in an intimidating interview. As an interviewer, it can feel like you're pulling teeth to get the person to talk to you. But Charmers are extroverted, so they open up easily and enjoy talking about themselves. Interviewers prefer to interview extroverts because it's easier.

When I started my career in recruiting, I would attend job fairs. Daylong events where I would meet over one hundred candidates. Back-to-back they would line up to talk to me about our open positions, and one by one they would sit down to answer my questions.

This is an especially hard interview environment. It's loud, it's chaotic, and a recruiter who you've never met before is asking you a bunch of questions at a rapid-fire pace. Then come the Charmers, and it's like night and day. Candidate after candidate may give you quick, short answers, leaving you feeling like they just want to get the hell out of there. But the Charmers love the questions, they love being there, and they love talking to you.

Before I identified the four interview styles, I thought all those other candidates that weren't enthusiastic must not be interested in the job or our company. It was my job to screen out the "bad" candidates so as to not waste my hiring manager's time. I passed only the ones who opened up on to the next round. It was my job to find the best, and it's easy to think Charmers are the best because they make a recruiter's job easy. (Now, I know what you're thinking: *It sure sounds like Charmers are the best at interviewing.* But I promise, Charmers have room for improvement too. Mike, a past client of mine, is a great example of this.)

Mike

A friend of a friend came to me to help him figure out a direction in his career. He always seemed to be doing a bunch of different things that all took him in different directions. Like me, he got his start in restaurants and knows what it means to hustle. He always has a smile on his face even when we talk about not-so-pleasant things. He is always optimistic and has a great sense of humor. He is a Charmer.

After working in fine dining, he got his Realtor's license and became a very successful broker, always topping the lists of most successful Realtors. When we met, he was years into a very prosperous real estate career, but he was also an artist, a producer, and a connector. He had his hands in everything. He knew a ton of people, and because of his personality, they would all bring him deals, projects, and opportunities to be involved with, and he wasn't one to say no. Finally, all that saying yes stretched him too thin and brought him to me.

With everything going on, he was lacking direction, and it was my job to help him figure out what he wanted. He didn't want to get out of real estate; it was too lucrative, and he had been doing it long enough that he could make the same money doing it part-time with his team. What he wanted to figure out was his next chapter. It was my job to help him see that, just as important as facilitating a reputation for being willing to help everyone, it was equally important for him to know who he was and what he wanted so he didn't fall off course. The idea of taking on his own career destiny so directly was foreign to him. He had always taken opportunities as they arose, never really thinking about whether they were good for him. He didn't think about where he wanted to go, so he wasn't worried about a particular path getting him to that final destination, his optimal place of success. He really liked the exciting beginning of things. That's why people came to him when they had an idea. He would share in their enthusiasm and get so energized that he would have to be a part of it. In interviews for business opportunities, he had a hard time saying no. It was almost impossible for him to tell someone something that they didn't want to hear.

When I would prepare him for interviews and meetings with potential investors, he would talk about how great the project could be, how amazing the opportunity, and how much money everyone would make. He lived in and talked about the future and possibilities. But investors live in numbers and data and quarterly projections. He was the idea man and often left out the important details.

He was inspirational. But knowing him, I knew that there was a dark side to that inspiration, an underside that few saw: knowing what others wanted came easy to him, but he didn't know what *he* wanted.

It was easy to be what everyone else wanted, and he liked doing it. He wasn't unhappy, but he knew that he could be happier and his career could have "a more linear direction." He was nearing fifty and wanted more stability. Figuring out his next step proved to be the hardest part. There was no shortage of opportunities coming his way. His issue, like most Charmers, was deciding what he wanted, not what others wanted.

This is not an uncommon story for Charmers. They are energized by others, and their need for connection can lead them to be caught up in ideas and dreams that are not necessarily their own. Mike was lacking direction because he had a hard time saying no, which is a danger of Charmer's accommodating nature. Part of Mike's issue as well was his reluctance to discuss the logistics of an idea. He, like other Charmers, enjoys talking about the exciting big picture, but forgets that the details are important too. This characteristic is most common for Charmers in interviews, when they may forgo adequately portraying their qualifications in service of connecting with the hiring manager. As was my approach with Mike, it's important that Charmers take time to reflect deeply on what they want, drawing connections to qualifications that they already have.

I also coached Mike on how to hire for his business. The same need to connect plagued him as a hiring manager. It was almost impossible for him to ask an interview question—"I just need to have a conversation, get to know them." I cautioned that this approach was not a good way to get to know someone for a professional opportunity. I challenged him, "If that's your strategy, how are you going to fairly compare candidates?" He said, "My gut feeling."

I warned Mike that your gut is not a good indicator of talent, particularly because bias could be involved. He persisted and made some hires based on feeling like he and the candidate could be friends. Though he wasn't sure of the candidate's qualifications, he was confident that their friendship would carry the relationship and motivate his new hires to learn anything that they didn't know.

Instead, it had the opposite effect, and his new employees saw him as a friend, not a boss. They took advantage, slacked off, and didn't do their jobs, let alone strive to learn anything new. They coasted. He grew bitter and didn't understand why his hiring practice wasn't working.

We took a few years off from coaching. He went to grad school and got busy building out some new real estate developments. He called me when one of his employees embezzled money. His way of interviewing hadn't worked. He found himself in one of the worst positions a hiring manager can find themselves in: disappointed in himself, questioning how it had all gone so bad, and ten steps behind because he'd lost a crucial member of his team.

How often have hiring managers made this mistake? In Mike's case it was extreme. But all too often, hiring managers miss red flags and issues because of a candidate's perceived likeability. Charmers believe that if an issue comes up, they can deal with it with the force of their personality, that their friendship, their history, will motivate the employee or protect themselves. They rationalize that if something goes wrong, they can talk some sense into the employee or, if it gets really bad, leverage their power and scare them into being a better employee. This assumption is often wrong and, given how costly the mistake was for Mike and how desperate he was to hire someone new, he was finally ready to listen.

As a Charmer, I could appreciate how hard it was for him to conduct structured interviews. I don't like them myself. But I encouraged him that if he tried, he'd make better hires and avoid the mistakes that he had just made.

We worked on balancing his need to be friendly and form a relationship in the interview with the practical questions of whether the candidate was qualified. He had been burned enough times with employees who weren't qualified that he was ready to ask tough technical questions. He admitted that it was not his favorite part and that it was hard for him. He didn't like playing the role of "mean teacher with a pop quiz." I could totally relate. We worked on it. He is still working on it.

For Charmer hiring managers like Mike, it's key to have standardized interview questions that you ask all candidates. This helps with your tendency to rely too heavily on relationship building and ensures that you focus on qualifications.

Mike is a classic example of a Charmer. He is so friendly and skilled at building relationships that interviewing with him, on either side of the table, is easy, even enjoyable. But he also demonstrates some of the traps that Charmers can fall into if they lack an awareness of their style.

Approach and Style

Charmers are highly accommodating and seek the approval of people that they meet. They want to be liked and want to form a connection. They are friendly and easy to talk to. It's hard not to like a Charmer in an interview. And that can also be their downfall.

When you prioritize making a connection and being liked, the performance in the interview is the most important thing. Charmers' need for approval drives them to make a great impression. They are not shallow. They don't lack substance. Just because they prioritize making a connection doesn't mean they don't come across as qualified or skilled. In fact, their need for approval drives them to do research, prepare, and often interview very well.

As a Charmer, when I was a candidate looking for jobs, I thought it was fun to do research on a company and then strategize the best way to position myself for the job. When I was on the other side of the table as a recruiter, I loved interviewing because I liked to strategize the best way to sell our company to each candidate. I loved being the corporate gatekeeper and the face of the company, hosting the candidate when they came to the office, selling them on our culture, and getting them to like me and thus the company. I had the same priority even though I now had all the power. I still wanted candidates to like me, and I wanted them to be likeable in the interview. And often the candidates I liked the most were the ones that liked me the most. If you want a Charmer to like you, tell them you like them.

Charmers believe that if they know the person they are interviewing with, they can better impress them by talking about things they care about. They are calculated. Charmers are accommodating and are happy to talk about your interests so that they may make a connection on a personal level that they then leverage into likeability. They create an air of friendliness and warmth.

Robert Greene describes Charmers in his book *The Art of Seduction*: "Their method is simple: They deflect attention from themselves and focus it on their target. They understand your spirit, feel your pain, adapt to your moods. In the presence of a Charmer you feel better about yourself. Charmers do not argue or fight, complain, or pester."

A client, Matt, whom I coached to get a competitive internship position, is a great example of this. He told me that when he met with the executive director of a global insurance brokerage, he noticed pictures of a little boy playing soccer on her desk. He asked, "Is that your son? What league does he play for?" She said, "Yes, he's fifteen now, but he played for the Lower Merion League." Matt had had a feeling and recognized the uniform in the picture, which was why he'd brought it up. "Wow, I coached that league in high school and I am going to referee for that program this summer. I've played soccer my whole life." The executive director was charmed, and they talked about soccer for the rest of the interview. He got the internship and went on to get hired full-time after graduation.

What Matt did is what a lot of Charmers do intuitively. They don't point at the picture and say, "Hey, I played for that league." Instead, they ask a question first to learn more information, to get you talking, to draw you in, and then they make the connection. When Charmers charm well, you don't even know it happened.

I vividly remember interviewing a candidate years ago who was a Charmer. When I greeted him in the lobby, he asked me how my day was. Often candidates are very nervous at the beginning of an interview, and when they ask you how you are doing, it comes across as rote small talk. They aren't listening to your answer, and it's okay—you know they're nervous and they'll warm up. This candidate was different. He was really listening. I recognized it immediately and was impressed. He was really interested in me. He wasn't asking how I was just because. He wanted to get to know me. There was a warmth. For a moment, I forgot I was in a position of power and he was applying for a job, and we transcended that artificial interaction. Charmers do that.

When Charmers use their charm poorly, their motives feel so obvious. Their need for approval comes across as desperation, and their eagerness pushes people away. They need to be liked and they want your approval, and they try really hard. When they do it well, it's great, but when they don't it comes off as disingenuous. The best of the best balance the Charmer traits. They use them wisely. They use their charm in the service of good. When Charmers interview well, they balance their need for approval with a self-assuredness; they aren't interviewing purely to be liked, and, ironically, that makes them more likeable. Charmers have a tendency to focus on telling stories and getting to know others, but an interview, remember, is not just an opportunity to connect; you also must show them how you can do the job. When a Charmer interviews well, they connect *and* explain their qualifications.

I was teaching hiring managers how to interview and a Charmer said, "When I go home after an interview and my husband asks me how it went, I say, 'Good, they liked me.'" Above all else, being liked is the most important thing to a Charmer, more than any other interview style. They are agreeable. They don't rock the boat or ask hard questions. They don't want to make anyone uncomfortable. They aren't seeking truth or data or trying to adapt. They just want to be liked.

This can come at a cost. With their singular focus on likeability, they can forget to talk about their qualifications. As we saw with Mike, Charmers are naturally great storytellers, but they can forget to provide real data and metrics to back up their stories. I can't tell you how many times I've had a great interview, yet when the candidate leaves, I am left feeling uncertain and wanting more. They told great stories, they were super personal, but I just wasn't sure. In debriefs with co-interviewers, the only thing we could put our finger on was that there was something missing. A hiring manager I used to interview with said it best about a Charmer after we had a great interview: "He's just an empty suit. Nice guy, but there's no *there* there."

On the other hand, when Charmers pay attention to the need to discuss qualifications, they can also be very good at using points of reference in the conversation to connect back to their experience and qualities that will make them a good fit for the job. They listen carefully for cues that they can use to connect what the interviewer says they want with who they are. They are always looking for a way to sell themselves, and they do it by rephrasing the interviewer's words and repeating them back. Because Charmers are externally focused, they adjust their answers and even their attitude using the verbal and nonverbal feedback they receive from the interviewer.

Charmers are also very enthusiastic and eager. They are a passionate bunch. But passion when not directed in a precise way can come across as too intense or vapid.

I once mock-interviewed a Charmer to prepare him for an interview, and I asked him a standard first interview question to build rapport. I said, "Why'd you go to Temple University and why'd you decide to major in risk management?" Most people talk for two to three minutes when they answer this question, but he talked and talked and talked. He told me his whole life story. I am really good at redirecting a lost candidate in an interview, but I couldn't get a word in edgewise. His answer went on for twenty minutes, the entire length of the mock interview. Charmers can talk, and they relish an opportunity to talk about themselves and tell their story, but they have to be sensitive to the need for concision.

Charmers take making an impression very seriously. It's a highly orchestrated event. They carefully curate what they will wear, say, and do. Charmers believe an interview is a show and they are showmen. And they believe that being liked is something they can control. In fact, they use the force of their personality to get someone to like them. It's a full-body assault. They use very confident body language: they sit on the edge of their seat and talk enthusiastically; they nod and smile. They show interest in the interviewer by being friendly, asking questions to find common ground, and they will even pay a compliment or tell a joke.

You can imagine how this plays out, right? Charmers who are genuine and have a high emotional intelligence know how to tell an appropriate, well-timed joke, whereas the less experienced Charmer may pay an inappropriate compliment. Years ago, I co-interviewed an applicant for a sales role with the head of HR. He was a Charmer who wasn't sophisticated. He made crude jokes, overly relied on telling stories that had no substance, and then to add insult to injury he winked at the head of HR—twice! Charmers must walk the fine line between being friendly and remaining professional.

Charmers make you feel like they are hanging on your every word. It's easy to talk to them and connect. One Charmer named

Jessica, whom I interviewed for an account manager position, was such a joy to interview, the interview lasted two hours. It was like meeting a new friend. Charmers do that.

Because they rely so heavily on making a connection and selling themselves by leveraging that connection, they really need a human interview and prefer unstructured interviews. For example, before setting up a live interview, sometimes a company sends a link to a platform where candidates can record answers to preset questions. This type of interview platform lacks intimacy. It's just you talking to yourself, being recorded and timed. No one performs particularly well on recorded screening interviews, but the artificial environment throws Charmers off especially as they need, above all else, someone to connect with.

What happens when there is a person or several people performing the interview, but they aren't willing to connect? In the same way that we are biased to our own interview style, we are also better at interviewing with someone who is our interview style. Makes sense, right? It's easier to talk to someone who is speaking your language. You will feel like you really clicked with that person or that the job is perfect for you when you interview with someone who is like you.

Charmers who interview with Charmers are going to feel like they met a new friend, the way I did so many years ago when I met Jessica. (We are still friends today.) Charmers want to "click," and when they do, they feel as though it is kismet. Meant to be because the conversation was so easy. When Charmers don't feel the "click," they think something is off. Must not be right. This often happens when they are interviewing someone who's their opposite style, an Examiner. Examiners don't prioritize making a connection in an interview; they prioritize getting it right. (More on Examiners in Chapter 9.)

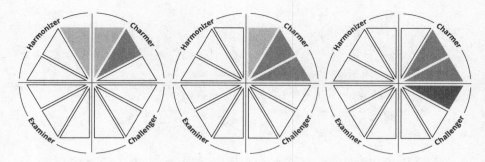

From left to right: Charmer with Harmonizer tendencies, Charmer, and Charmer with Challenger tendencies

Charmer Variations

Like all interview styles, there is variation within the Charmer. As you can see in the interview style hexagon, Charmers are closest to Harmonizers and Challengers, and often share traits with these styles.

TRAITS CHARMERS SHARE WITH HARMONIZERS

- *People-focused*
- *Externally focused*
- *Accommodating and flexible*
- *Charming*
- *Know how their personality fits into the company culture*
- *Believe anyone can be persuaded, and live by the motto* charm works
- *Make a good impression by being friendly, likeable, and relatable.*
- *Comfortable with ambiguity, can improvise*
- *Comfortable selling oneself*
- *Confidence comes from social desirability*
- *Like small talk and conversation*

- *Can change style and answers to fit others*
- *Rely on soft skills*
- *Don't like when the interview is only technical*
- *Need chitchat to break tension and decrease their nerves. Need rapport to put them at ease.*

TRAITS CHARMERS SHARE WITH CHALLENGERS

- *Answers are expansive*
- *Solve problems by talking them out*
- *Handle personality questions well*
- *Open up easily, use personal stories to illustrate experiences, including goals and failures*
- *Can and will lead a conversation no matter what the power dynamic—candidate or hiring manger*

Because of this overlap, in addition to the Charmer style, there are also two variations of Charmers: Charmer/Harmonizer and Charmer/Challenger. Let's look a bit closer at what differentiates the three types of Charmers.

Charmer with Harmonizer Tendencies

Charmer/Harmonizers are extroverted with introverted tendencies. They are the quietest Charmer, and the most willing to adapt of any style. When they are not in a setting that calls for them to be outgoing, they prefer to be quiet. They have a tendency to balance out the interviewer. For example, if they are being interviewed by an extrovert, they may become more introverted and vice versa.

Charmers with Harmonizer tendencies let the more dominant personality take the lead. They hold back and observe the conversation until something piques their interest, speaking up if the topic interests them. They do not steer the conversation to them or change the subject if it doesn't interest them; context has to be right for them to seek attention. Charmer/Harmonizers charm by being thoughtful.

Charmer

A Charmer (without any variation) is extroverted and accommodating. Charmers are energized by other people; they open up easily and like to share details about themselves. Of all the interview styles, Charmers like interviews the most because they like to showcase who they are and what they can do. They prefer unstructured interviews that feel conversational. Charmers need small talk and time to get to know the other person. They speak to think, so Charmers don't require a script or talking points; talking and thinking on their feet are two of their biggest strengths. Charmers are externally focused, taking their cues on how to behave from others. They change their interview answers depending on the cues they receive from the interviewees, and they are comfortable adapting to the energy in the room and to the needs of their audience. Charmers charm by being eager, flexible, and entertaining.

Charmer with Challenger Tendencies

A Charmer/Challenger is extroverted but less accommodating than a Charmer or Charmer/Harmonizer because they are more steadfast. A Charmer who shares traits with a Challenger is accommodating, but only to a point. They are extroverted, so interviews energize them, and they take their cues from the interviewer, but when it comes to answering interview questions about their qualifications and other technical questions, unlike Charmers, their answers don't change based on what they think the other person wants to hear. A Charmer with Challenger tendencies is the most bold of the Charmers. They are undeterred in their approach, and feel as though they can persuade, convince, and cajole an interviewer by being persistent, thorough, and undaunted. Charmers with Challenger tendencies charm with toughness, persuasion, and a little force.

Key Takeaways

How to Tell If You Are Talking to a Charmer

- They open up easily.

- They enjoy talking about themselves.

- They are good storytellers.

- They are friendly and want to make a personal connection.

- They are not afraid to put it all out there if it helps them succeed at their goal.

- They view interviewing as a performance.

- They nod and smile and engage with their whole body.

- Charmers get you to see them as qualified by being eager.

(For practice identifying the different styles, see the Deciphering the Interview Styles activity in the Appendix.)

Strengths and Overused Strengths

Charmers have many strengths, but when they are out of balance, their intentions can be misinterpreted. The following table looks at their strengths and how those strengths can appear when they are overused.

Strengths	Overused Strengths
Enthusiastic	Overly eager, tending to look vapid
Engaging	Too much emphasis on the conversation
Approval seeking	Lose sight of the bigger picture
Confident	Bulldozer
Willing	Desperate
Personable	Focus too heavily on the connection, not enough on their qualifications
Showmen	Lacking substance
Storyteller	They can be exhausting, talking in circles without making their point

Interviewing with a Charmer

harmers are accommodating. They participate in what psychologists call catering behaviors. They cater to others' interests and expectations by intentionally minimizing their own preferences. Catering means you put the imagined needs in front of your own. You assume that you should act a certain way to make a good impression, and therefore you don't act authentically.

Much in the same way that the Charmer interview style is the one that is preferred by society, a lot of interview advice is geared toward catering behaviors. There is an assumption of how we should act and what we should say in an interview, and most interview advice focuses on how to fit within that box.

As a Charmer client who sought the approval of the interviewers put it, "I wouldn't be my true self in an interview. I wasn't pretending to be something I am not. I was the professional version of me. The all-buttoned-up, say-the-right-things, leave-out-parts-of-the-story version of me. Whatever I thought would make a good impression."

This approach often works, because it makes a good impression, but there is generally a cost, namely that we minimize pieces of ourselves in service of aligning with others. But catering behaviors are based on assumptions we make of others' expectations, not facts. So we contort ourselves to imaginary needs.

What if I were to tell you to imagine what a hiring manager wants, and then I told you to change your behavior to fit what you imagined? When we intellectually think about what we unconsciously do, it sounds ludicrous, right?

Even if you knew, factually, what that person wanted to hear, pretending to be something you're not or highlighting parts of yourself that aren't normally prominent doesn't pay off in the long term. Because eventually you will be yourself at the job, and you might find that it isn't right for who you actually are, just for who you were pretending to be in the interview. In your quest for approval, you may even find yourself overlooking red flags that point to issues like toxic work environments. Another Charmer client of mine said, "I thought the goal of the interview was to get the job. Years later, after a few bad jobs, I realized that it isn't about getting any job—it's about getting the right job."

Yes, an interview is supposed to find out if you're right for the role, but it is also about you figuring out which role is right for you. If you want lasting success, both of these things need to align, and if you make an effort to remain your authentic self in interviews, you'll be more likely to find a job where they do.

Even though we think we make a better impression when we cater to others, there is research that says we make a better impression by simply being ourselves. This is contrary to all the popular interview advice out there, and contrary to a Charmer's natural tendency. For Charmers especially, the approach is never "I am just going to be myself and see what happens." Instead, they are always accommodating others' needs to gain their approval.

Why Charmers Seek Approval

Humans are relational; we all want to be liked, we want others to accept us, and we want to belong. To varying degrees, we all seek approval. When there is a job or a promotion on the line, our innate need to be liked comes out. Some seek approval more than others, and this difference is apparent in interviews. Of the four interview styles, Charmers and Harmonizers are the most approval seeking. Charmers believe they will make the best impression by being likeable, friendly, and charming. They seek approval of the person interviewing them by being friendly.

Charmers want to be validated by other people. They need an audience. All Charmers, on some level, are looking for validation because they can't provide it to themselves. They are externally motivated, so to some degree, Charmers get the validation they crave by getting the job or landing the promotion.

Charmers put extraordinary efforts into the whole interview, the impression they make, and how they make people feel. They trade in emotional currency easily. They are perceptive and know what people want to hear, and they also know how they need to hear it. Charmers are great at delivering tough subjects and information indirectly as to not put the other person on the defense. Unlike the other styles, Charmers are the most diplomatic and the most effective emotional negotiators. They disarm by using acceptance, reassurance, and compliments. They believe that creating a sense of warmth and connection will get someone to open up and like them faster than any other strategy. They therefore don't speak from a place of perfection but own up to their own shortcomings and easily talk about their weaknesses. Charmers easily give someone else credit, soften to other people's views, and are agreeable.

Charmers are willing to tell white lies in service of the greater truth and greater good. They are willing to say what someone wants to hear to save their feelings because above all else they want others to feel good. They believe if someone feels good, then that good feeling will extend to them and they will ultimately reap the rewards. They also do not mind if someone tells them a white lie in an interview; they expect it—they see it as protecting them and part of the process. They do not like heroic truth telling the way a Challenger does. Charmers, on the other hand, appreciate and see value in emphasizing the things that make people feel good, not to deceive them but to cement what's most important to them: a positive interaction and being seen as likeable. They will say the office is nice, the coffee is good, and the work looks interesting. They do not value totally accurate accounts if those accounts would hurt someone's feelings or push them away. They resist some facts. And expect others to do the same.

How Charmers Can Manage Their Need for Approval

While they are very diplomatic, Charmers have a tendency to overly prioritize others.

I have seen many clients over the years become more confident through the interview prep process. Just the acts of writing their resume, thinking about their work experience, and practicing answers to interview questions make them see how they are qualified rather than feeling like they have something to prove. What they have done, where they have come from, and how they have grown are extremely important things to think about during interview prep for Charmers.

 INTERVIEW PRINCIPLE FOR JOB SEEKERS

The act of creating a resume, thinking about your work experience, and practicing answers to interview questions can help build your self-awareness and confidence, so you interview better.

Charmers can work on being more secure and self-accepting. To do so, think about your qualifications, what you have to offer, and your whole story. Once you are proud of yourself and feel confident in what you have to offer, you won't need other people's approval. It's always good to remember that, as Lao Tzu says, "Because one believes in oneself, one doesn't try to convince others."

Believe in yourself and know who you are. That is a recipe for the perfect interview!

Empowerment is one part believing in yourself and one part having the skills that it takes.

Charmers have an opposite that they can look to for inspiration. When it comes to managing their need for approval and pulling back on the reins of their eagerness and passion, they should look to Examiners. Examiners are private and focused on giving verifiable, factual answers that are consistent.

Learn to welcome criticism as feedback, not disapproval. Disagreement is not a form of hostility—you can like someone and still disagree with them. Being liked is not dependent on constant agreement. If you are really listening to someone, you will see that you don't agree with everything, and that is okay. Growth comes when we are uncomfortable.

Give yourself the approval you want others to give you. It's a flimsy and insecure place to be, wishing for someone else to give you what you want and need. It also gives others all the power. Instead, give it to yourself. In this case, work on your resume, have a mock interview, record yourself, and play it back. Use the STAR method to create answers to common behavioral questions, and in telling and retelling your work history you will gain confidence.

 INTERVIEW PRINCIPLE FOR JOB SEEKERS

Use the STAR method to create answers to common behavioral questions.

SITUATION: Describe the situation you were in or a task that you needed to accomplish. Use a real-life example from a job, class, or volunteer experience and be specific.

TASK: Clearly define the goal you were working toward in that situation.

ACTION: The interviewer wants to hear what *you* did. Use the word *I*, along with powerful action words.

RESULT: Describe what happened and how you were responsible for it. This is your time to shine! The story should showcase how you were the hero—how you retained the tough customer, or finished the project ahead of schedule, or saved the company $40,000. Most of the time, candidates leave the interviewer hanging, so always give the result without having to be asked. Don't be shy! An interview is the time and place to talk about your successes.

> If you have a tendency to talk too much (or not enough), then this formula will keep you on track.
>
> For an interviewer, using the STAR method means asking about specific situations using behavioral questions like, "Describe a situation in which you were able to use persuasion to successfully convince someone to see things your way," and step by step, using a real-life example, please tell me how you delegated responsibilities on a project and how a candidate handled it.

Not all rejection is bad. Many Charmers learn this the hard way. You can charm your way into almost any job, but remember, it's not about getting any job, it's about finding the right one. Defining success for yourself is a good first step.

A good therapist or coach can help you see how seeking approval is holding you back and help you establish a secure sense of self, healthy boundaries, and a life built to make you proud, not others.

When Charmers Interview Well

Charmers can be smooth and savvy. They generate a feeling of warmth and connection. They get to know you by asking insightful questions and making you feel comfortable. Unlike other styles, who ask questions for other reasons, a Charmer asks questions to get to know you because they genuinely care about you. They believe the best way to be liked is to show an interest in someone else. We like people who are curious about us. We want to open up and share with people who open up and share about themselves.

When Charmers interview well, they balance their need for approval with confidence that comes from knowing who they are, what they do, and how they are qualified.

They interview well when they know themselves and can easily sell themselves by explaining how and why they are a good fit. A Charmer pinpoints exactly what the hiring manager needs, and since they know themselves so well, they can articulate their transferable skills in a way that the hiring manager leaves the interview confident that they can do the job.

Charmers are very good at making a connection, but to be good at interviews you need to not only be likeable, you must also be technically capable. You must be able to talk about how you are qualified using metrics and examples of your work. Again, the STAR method is a great way to do this. Report your abilities, don't just connect.

When Charmers Interview Poorly

When a Charmer interviews poorly, it's often because they are overly relying on their ability to talk. They talk too much and make it all about them. Their ability to entertain can turn into a one-man show. They can oversell, finish people's sentences, and bulldoze the conversation. While it's great that Charmers are expressive, this can come across as overconfidence.

Charmers also over-rely on gaining the approval of others. I worked with a Charmer hiring manager whose need to gain everyone's approval was oppressive. It dominated every conversation he had. He told stories that he thought made him look cool, but instead of sounding interesting, he just came across as insecure. His need to be liked had the opposite effect. It pushed people away. When Charmers are too focused on gaining others' approval, instead of creating a feeling of mutual connection, they just come across as needy.

When a Charmer interviews poorly often it comes from a place of needing approval, needing to be liked, and wanting to make a connection. One of the best qualities of Charmers is their level of enthusiasm and interest in the job. But the dark side is the potential of coming across as desperate.

I worked with a client who came to me because he couldn't get past the first few interviews. He hired me to mock-interview him and tell him what he was doing wrong and help him figure out why he kept getting passed over. I asked a few standard interview questions, and there it was, plain as day: he was incredibly needy. In fact, he told me that he prided himself on the fact that at the end of every interview he made a point to ask, "Is there anything I shared today that would give you pause or reservations about hiring me?" On the surface this is a fine question to ask, but when it's combined with a Charmer's need for approval it comes across as awkward and intense. And here's the thing: hiring managers and HR people are not trained to give you feedback; they aren't coaches, so they won't answer this question honestly anyway.

 INTERVIEW PRINCIPLE FOR JOB SEEKERS

Hiring managers and HR people are not trained to give you feedback on your interview. If you need feedback, it's best to hire a coach who can work with you to improve.

A Charmer can interview poorly when they are overly friendly. Endorsing everything someone says, lavishing compliments, and laughing too hard at every joke can be as off-putting as being rude. When Charmers interview poorly, it's because they are too agreeable. They agree with everything you say. When you say something clever, they are thrilled; when you say something dumb, they are equally thrilled. They are overly eager, overly supportive, overly considerate. They provide blanket praise and compliments that miss the mark. They so badly want to make the other person feel good, but their eagerness comes across as fake or insincere. They are too upbeat, too thoughtful, and too interested, making us feel that it comes across as inauthentic. To interview better, they need to be more discerning in their praise as to maintain the currency of their compliments and excitement. Again, this comes down to authenticity. Don't say something just because you think someone wants to hear it; only say what you mean.

When a Charmer interviews poorly they forget themselves entirely. They forget that they won't have something in common with everyone and that it's okay to disagree and offer a different viewpoint. In fact, the person you are interviewing with may indeed be looking for you to offer your opinion, challenge the status quo, and push back. Being perfectly agreeable doesn't mean you will get hired; in fact, it might be the very reason you don't get hired.

Charmers have to acknowledge that they may displease some and learn to be okay with that.

The risk of being overly friendly means that you are going to be everywhere and nowhere. There is an inherent risk in being ourselves: some people might not like you, and that's okay! When a Charmer interviews poorly, it is often because they have contorted themselves to fit an idea of what they think society and others want them to be. In the process, they risk losing themselves.

How to Interview a Charmer Job Seeker

Charmers believe that they will get the internship, job, or promotion because they are likeable. In order to create that likeability, Charmers must build rapport first, which allows them to modify their answers. They sell themselves by altering their answers and attitudes to fit the person they are interviewing with.

As a job seeker, they are put off by tough questions that happen too early in an interview. Rapport is essential for a Charmer. Charmers prefer unstructured interviews; they love to just have a conversation, but the research is very clear that structured interviews lead to better results. So tell all candidates that you will be conducting a structured interview, which means asking everyone the same interview questions. This makes it easier to debrief and compare different candidates. It also decreases bias.

 INTERVIEW PRINCIPLE FOR HIRING MANAGERS

Structured interviews, where you ask the same questions of each candidate, are a great way to decrease bias in the interview process.

To get to the heart of the matter and pin down a Charmer, you should ask them specific questions about a situation. For example, since Charmers like to focus on the good parts, ask them, "Walk me through your biggest failure, what you learned, and how you dealt with it?"

An unprepared Charmer prefers generalities and likes to keep it vague if they can. Ask behavioral questions, using the STAR method technique, informing the Charmer candidate that you're looking to find out more information about their motivation and thought process. Ask specific questions about how many times they did something, ask for data, and encourage them to walk you through how they do their job using facts, figures, and details.

How to Interview with a Charmer Hiring Manager

Charmers are focused mostly on making a connection. If you are being interviewed by a Charmer hiring manager, make an effort to connect to them. This starts with small talk and asking how they are; resist your urge to dive right into the specifics. As hiring managers, Charmers are put off by a candidate who asks tough or difficult questions without first getting to know them, so wait to ask your questions until you have established a rapport.

According to the Equal Employment Opportunity Commission (EEOC), which is responsible for laws removing bias from the hiring process, an interview is a test and should be conducted like one, with set questions and a time limit. Charmer hiring managers are not good at this. In fact, this is the hardest thing for Charmer hiring managers to overcome because they prioritize liking the applicant and wanting to work with them. It doesn't mean that they don't care if the candidates are qualified, but they prioritize a connection over qualification. For example, if you're an Examiner in interviews, your priority is to be seen as qualified; therefore, you may have to recast some of the examples that you use to get someone to see you as qualified and make them into stories using the STAR method.

A Charmer hiring manager will overlook issues in deference to how likeable a person is. They are blinded by liking someone, and worse, if someone lavishes them with praise and compliments them, they are even more likely to ignore red flags. Praise and compliments are kryptonite for a Charmer. If you want a Charmer hiring manager to like you, just tell them that you like them, that you are impressed with who they are and what they've built.

I worked with a large restaurant that was having a lot of turnover in the host position. They assumed they were hiring the wrong people. I assumed it was how they were interviewing. I consulted with them and then shadowed them in three back-to-back interviews. The general manager and assistant manager conducted the interviews, and because they are in the hospitality industry, they were very friendly. They had a conversation with the candidates, and wanted them to feel comfortable. They didn't ask any traditional interview questions; they simply inquired about start dates and availability. When the candidates left, I said, "You need to be a whole lot tougher. You just talked to those candidates like they were customers. Interviewing is going to require you to change up your approach and tone because you need to ask questions." They were shocked but also relieved. The next round of interviews, they shadowed me, and I showed them how to balance likeability and getting their questions answered. Then we had a few more sessions to create better interview questions, and they practiced.

As a Charmer hiring manager, it is your natural inclination to want to be liked and to like the other person, but that can get in your way. You need to set that aside so you can first figure out if this candidate is even qualified. Once you figure out they are qualified, then you can think about their likeability.

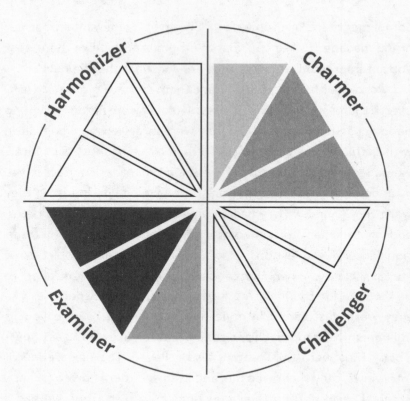

How a Charmer Interviews with Their Opposite—The Examiner

When a Charmer interviews with their opposite, the Examiner, they may feel that they are preoccupied with how they do their job, what their qualifications are, and their weaknesses. They may also feel that they didn't have an opportunity to connect on an interpersonal level because Examiners are more task focused. Examiners are more private and, unlike Charmers, do not use personal conversations to connect when first meeting people. They are slower to warm up, and therefore, giving them space to do so on their own timeline and respecting their privacy is a better tactic than trying to connect right away. Charmers generally rely on telling stories and their ability to connect, but when interviewing with an Examiner, it's better to focus more on the results of your work and use metrics instead of vague language.

Charmers should slow down their tone and pace when meeting with an Examiner.

Charmers should use their ability to flex their style to adapt to others' needs. Tap into what the Examiner expects and change your approach to meet them where they are.

How You Can Balance Your Approach and Tap into the Other Styles

Charmers can be more successful if they pull traits from other styles to balance out their natural tendencies:

- *Charmers can borrow the steadfastness from Challengers and not worry so much about being liked but instead be themselves.*
- *Charmers can take the more businesslike approach of Examiners and highlight their qualifications as much as their likeability.*
- *Charmers can learn more about their audience if they employ Harmonizer tendencies and ask more questions about how they would fit into the culture as opposed to selling the company on them.*

Advice for Charmers	**Pre-interview Mantras for Charmers to Manage Their Need to Be Liked**
It pays to be yourself.	"Balance charisma and qualifications." "Balance your need to be liked with showing them how you are qualified." "It's okay to not be liked by everyone."

Key Takeaways for Charmer Job Seekers

- Telling someone what they want to hear is not a good strategy long term. You may land the job, but you can't pretend forever, and when you stop, you might find that the job is not right for you.

- Don't let yourself become so distracted by making a connection that you forget to discuss your qualifications. Relationships are important, but skills matter too.

Key Takeaways for Charmer Hiring Managers

- A structured interview leads to better results and allows you to compare candidates more easily.

- You will be attracted to candidates who you like; fight this urge. Rather, you want to hire someone who can do the job. Don't over-rely on how much you like the candidate.

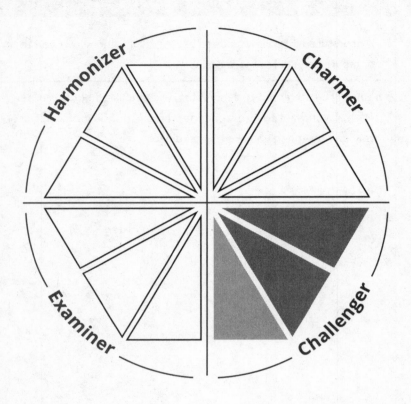

Challenger. Interesting and thought-provoking, they open up in interviews and pride themselves on being truthful. They are focused internally and are not eager to please. They are outgoing and enjoy providing a new perspective. They will make the interviewer think. They push boundaries and are often introspective. They come across as undaunted and perseverant. They are not overly concerned with getting the interviewer to like them. Their top priority is to be themselves. They want to feel heard. They may be suspicious of anyone who is overly friendly, and they may even be skeptical of charm.

7

Challenger

"I want to be me."

I have taught interview skills to college students since 2011; every Wednesday, Friday, and Saturday I taught a three-hour interview skills workshop. (I have taught over five hundred of these workshops.) In almost every workshop, there's always one person who thinks that the class is going to be a waste of their time. I spot them right away. When we are waiting for everyone to show up and I am setting up, they are the ones asking the people around them, "Is this really three hours?" They sigh. They fidget. They are annoyed. If the person sitting next to them doesn't agree with them, they talk louder, turn around in their seats, and look for anyone in the room to recruit to be disgruntled with them.

I love these students. I am not a skeptic, but you need one in the classroom, and I am always glad they are there. They fulfill an important function in the learning ecosystem. As the instructor, I like to teach to the skeptic. The skeptic is always the hardest person to convince, so when I'm able to get them on board, I know I've done my job. For the students, the skeptic will ask the tough questions and put themselves out there in a way that most students won't, making the class more engaging.

During one workshop, a skeptical student started in right before I began to teach, claiming that he didn't need to attend the class, that he already knew how to interview. According to him, interviewing is "not really a thing I can explain you just do it in the moment, ya know?"

What he and most skeptics were getting at is another pervasive myth about interviewing that I would like to dispel before we go any further: That interviewing isn't something you can prepare for. That you'll do better on the spot because you'll sound scripted if you prepare.

In all the years I have taught people to interview, I have never seen anyone do better "on the spot." It's a myth that people tell themselves to get out of doing the hard work. To get out of preparing. Like most myths, it sounds good. "I have to be in the interview to answer these questions." "I don't want to sound scripted." Over the years, so many people have told me this, and every time I say, "Okay, show me what you got." And I ask the most basic interview question, "Tell me about yourself." And they stumble and they blather and they repeat themselves, and then they apologize because they realize that they aren't great on the spot.

If you can't perform well in a mock interview, you aren't going to do well in a real interview. Interviewing is like anything else: you must practice to get better at it. If you can't make the shot during practice, the likelihood of you sinking it with the pressure of the clock, opponents, and a crowd is slim to none. All great athletes practice. Great hiring managers are great at interviews because they have done it over and over. I got good at interviews simply because I had a lot of experience doing them. The more you interview, the better you'll be. Practice truly does make perfect.

INTERVIEW PRINCIPLE FOR HIRING MANAGERS

Hiring managers have less experience than job seekers, and 90 percent are untrained to interview. You are *not* bad at interviewing, you're just unprepared.

Challengers often have trouble with practice. Above all, they want to be themselves, and they feel that practicing can make the interview feel forced and inauthentic. Challengers often push back on the idea of practicing, just as the student in my class did. But confidence comes from practice. I have coached clients who told me they should've done this work ten years ago. I have worked with hiring managers with thirty-plus years of experience who had to learn it the hard way. I have worked with college students who tell me that discovering who they are and figuring out how to talk about themselves was the most beneficial thing they did in college. It takes work, but it's worth it.

Challengers See Interviews as an Investigation

Of all the interview styles, Challengers prioritize being themselves. They are courageous. They pride themselves on speaking up. They value integrity.

Unlike Charmers, who seek approval, Challengers seek respect. They want to be themselves and they want to be heard. Challengers show they are qualified by asking tough questions. They look at an interview like a debate or cross-examination.

Challengers understand something better than the other styles, which is, it doesn't pay to pretend to be something you're not. Many of them have told me that it feels impossible to pretend. I once taught a Challenger who told me, "I feel constrained by integrity." That's because Challengers are steadfast. Once they commit to an answer that feels authentic to them, they will stay the course. Challengers are going their way whether you're on board or not. Interviewing them feels like that sometimes: they are happy to take the lead, and often you can feel like you are there to answer their questions and get out of their way.

A few years ago, I met L. Wayne Hoover, Certified Forensic Interviewer (CFI), at a Society for Human Resource Management (SHRM) conference. When I introduced myself to him, I said, "I specialize in teaching people how to interview." He said, "Me too." I was thrilled! I had never met anyone else who specializes in teaching people how to interview. He lifted up his backpack to show me the proof. Emblazoned on the front was the logo of his organization, Wicklander-Zulawski & Associates, the world-leader in investigative interview training: *The Training That Gets the Truth*. We hit it off immediately.

Wayne is a senior partner at Wicklander-Zulawski & Associates; before that, he was the police commissioner in the Chicago area. He is also the chair of International Association of Interviewers (IAI). We spent the next two hours talking about interviewing. He was an interrogator and is one of the preeminent teachers in the world on investigative interviewing techniques. His organization is hired to consult with forensic companies, and they hold seminars all over the world on how to conduct investigative interviews. Part of their suite of services is teaching hiring managers how to interview using similar interviewing techniques that they teach police officers and detectives, providing investigators in loss prevention, human resources, operations, and more with morally, legally, and ethically acceptable methods for obtaining the truth in the workplace.

I picked Wayne's brain on interrogation techniques, and he told me story after story. I shared my corporate perspective, and we made each other think. I respect him greatly, and we formed a fast friendship. A few months after meeting, I sent him and his partner our interview style assessment, and, as predicted, he was a Challenger.

Challengers believe in getting to the truth. Just like Wayne's corporate logo. They are skeptical and they go into an interview believing that a job seeker or hiring manager is leaving something out, and it's their job to get to the bottom of it.

As a person, Wayne is respectful. He is warm and kind, but not for a second did I think he totally trusted me yet. There wasn't a moment of hesitation in him getting to know me. I felt a little on edge, like I was being studied. Like I better answer his questions right or he'd see right through me. He wasn't aggressive at all. He was smooth. As he said, he relied on the system; it was a way of asking questions in a certain order to get someone to reveal themselves and their truth. A Challenger through and through.

Julia

I worked with a client, Julia, who is an attorney. She had vast experience as a prosecutor and a litigator in both criminal and civil cases. She came to me to prepare for an upcoming interview for a judgeship. In her county, a position like this only opens up every ten years or so. Nine years prior, she had interviewed for a family court judgeship, and didn't get it because of her performance in the interview. She didn't want that to happen again.

In our first session, she told me that she didn't like to prepare for interviews because she didn't want to feel scripted. I had heard that before. I asked her, "Do you prepare for a trial?" She said, "Of course." I said, "Why is this any different?" She paused. "Well, I don't want to prepare because I don't like talking about myself."

Part of preparing for an interview is getting your mindset right.

It's a head game. What Julia needed to get comfortable with was talking about herself, but even deeper, she needed to see herself worthy of the position she was interviewing for. Once she got there, she was able to start preparing to sell herself.

Most clients that don't like to "sell themselves" tell me it's because it feels like bragging. An interview can be a stage, or an isolation booth, or a torture chamber, depending on your mindset. If you go into it thinking that you are being forced to sell yourself, it will affect your performance. Instead, shift your mindset to something that makes you more comfortable. Instead of thinking about selling yourself, imagine you're a product. You aren't selling yourself; you are selling the solution to their problem. Every hiring manager has a problem: they have an opening, and they need someone to fill it. They need a solution to their problem. Take *you* out of the equation. Be the solution. This trick has worked for many clients, Challenger or not.

Once we tackled that, we were ready to dissect what happened when she bombed the interview years before.

"What happened nine years ago? Why do you think the interview didn't go well?" She said, "When I got to the municipal building where the interviews were being held, I ran into someone in the parking lot and they said, 'You're the best candidate; it's yours to lose.' Then I walked in to check in and they were running behind. They put me in a little file room to wait for my interview, and I waited two hours. The whole time I just psyched myself out."

Answering questions about the law and her ability to manage a courtroom was easy for Julia. The technical stuff she had down pat, but what she hadn't thought about or planned for was the *why you?* question, because she didn't want to talk about herself. She looked at the interview as an inquiry into her technical aptitude, and when she had two hours to sit and wonder why she was the best candidate, doubt crept in.

In the interview, the interviewer asked her, "Why are you applying for family court? Your resume and application look like you'd be perfect for Superior Court. If we give you this judgeship, are you just going to apply for a Superior Court position when one opens up?" For Challengers, it is really hard to give a diplomatic answer to questions like this since integrity is so important to them; the first answer that comes to mind for them is the truth. In Julia's case she said, "Yes, I will apply for a Superior Court position." Sure, this was the truth, but a more diplomatic answer would've been, "As you can see on my resume and application, I have vast experience and that is what I believe would make me the best family court judge, and here is why . . ." Challengers don't do that. Julia answered the question directly, and they passed on her for the judgeship and gave it to another woman. Needless to say, for her next interview we worked on her diplomacy and practiced answering questions indirectly while positioning herself for the job that she wanted.

Approach and Style

Challengers are internally focused. They don't adjust their answers or their attitude using the verbal and nonverbal feedback they receive from the interviewer. Often they come into an interview with an answer in mind, and they don't change it. Whereas Charmers and Harmonizers will adapt quickly in the moment and change their answers, Challengers do not.

Embedded in the core of a Challenger is a need to be heard. In the way that Charmers make it easy to interview them, Challengers make it, well, challenging. But that is their charm. Challengers show their value by sharing new ideas, poking holes, and asking questions. We need people to ask tough questions; we need the skeptics and the nonbelievers. The world needs people who are constrained by integrity, people who are not afraid to bring up tough subjects and press on.

In an interview setting, being straightforward can be off-putting. A Challenger's desire to be clear and put it all out there can prevent them from being diplomatic and making the best impression, as it did with Julia.

I interviewed a candidate at the beginning of my HR career, when I was fresh out of college, and he started by interrupting me and asked me what my qualifications were. I suppose at the heart of it he didn't want to be asked questions that I couldn't also answer. Challengers need an element of fairness, equity, and balance. If it doesn't feel fair for a Challenger, it's hard for them to proceed. Challengers need justification.

Challengers are extroverted, so they open up easily. But they don't necessarily like to talk about themselves in the way that a Charmer does.

A Challenger's interview answers can be direct, no-nonsense, and firm. There are times, however, when that can hurt them. Their honesty can get in their way.

Challengers are skeptical of charm. As job seekers they are pre-occupied with "getting down to it" or "figuring it out." Since integrity is so important to them, a critical element of an interview is getting to the truth. They aren't impressed by small talk, rapport building, or stories. They want to get into the nitty-gritty. They want to hear about the skeletons in the closet. They do not shy away from uncomfortable subjects, which can be a problem if improperly timed. I mock-interviewed a client once to prepare him for an interview with a large insurance broker that had just rebranded. I asked a few standard interview questions, and then he interjected, "Can you tell me the company's plan to repair its reputation?" I believe there is a time and place for this question—fifteen minutes into an interview is not it.

A Challenger's need for the truth is their best quality. They want answers, and they want to give their opinion. A Challenger sees an interview as their opportunity to be heard. They want to use it to talk about their concerns and any issues that they might have. Challengers sell themselves by sharing their ideas and experience and asking tough questions.

Challengers speak to think, which means they need to talk to formulate their ideas, but they also think it's unprofessional to express a half-thought idea, so they can be long-winded at times. When I coach a Challenger, like Julia, I encourage them to take time to think about their answers ahead of time, so they make their point before losing their audience. This was especially key for Julia, who was headed into a timed panel interview with a lot on the line, so there was little room for her to figure her answers out on the spot.

Unlike Charmers, they are not focused on getting you to like them. They are focused on being straightforward and acting with integrity. If you like them, that's a bonus. When you interview them, it can feel like you aren't making a connection unless you are sufficiently answering their questions. The back-and-forth of questions, not small talk, is the way that Challengers build rapport.

I got a call from a frantic woman on a Sunday. She told me that she had been interviewing for a while and just couldn't land a job. She had to talk to me ASAP because she had a final interview coming up and needed my help. We scheduled a time and had a session. I asked her a few questions; she was brusque. Her answers were decisive and not in a good way. She had decided and that was that. She lacked sensitivity, tact, or finesse. She got right to the point, blunt and matter-of-fact.

Her answers left me feeling like her intent was to make me feel inferior and stupid. Her goal was to show her superiority by spouting off what she knew. My job as her coach was to gently show her this and how it might not be in her best interest to tackle it that way. And *tackle* was the best way to describe it. It felt physical.

When I mirrored back to her what she was doing, there was a long pause. Then she said, "Oh my God, I'm a jerk." I carefully said, "It's okay. You're not a jerk. It's just the way you answered the questions. I can help. Let's think of a way for you to soften your approach, but it still feels authentically you."

She is an extreme example. As a coach, I could see past her brusque exterior because it's my job to help a client sell themselves. But as a hiring manager, I wouldn't have hired her. I wouldn't have liked her.

After I identified the four interview styles, it made coaching so much easier. I was able to easily identify what someone's priority was in an interview, and I was able to give them constructive feedback more quickly. Through knowledge of my clients' interview styles, I understood their natural tendencies and therefore could give them feedback and help them align their interview answers with who they really are. In this client's case, I knew that if I had told her to "just be nicer" or to "tell them what they want to hear," she wouldn't have done it, and she wouldn't have taken me seriously because a Challenger needs to be themselves no matter what. Traditional interview advice would be to tell her to act differently. But we spend a lot of our lives being told to improve our weaknesses as opposed to using our strengths. As is stated in StrengthsFinder, "people have several times more potential for growth when they invest their energy in developing their strengths instead of correcting their deficiencies."

And I want Challengers to be themselves; I want *everyone* to lean into their strengths, to identify what's working and use that. We often rely too much on our natural tendencies; we can be overly charming or overly challenging. The goal is to find the balance.

From left to right: Challenger with Charmer tendencies, Challenger, and Challenger with Examiner tendencies

Challenger Variations

Like all interview styles, there is variation within the Challenger style. As you can see in the interview style hexagon, Challengers are closest to Charmers and Examiners, and often share traits with these styles.

TRAITS CHALLENGERS SHARE WITH CHARMERS

- *Answers are expansive*
- *Solve problems by talking them out*
- *Handle personality questions well*
- *Open, use personal stories to illustrate experiences, share failures and goals easily*
- *Speak to think*
- *Can and will lead a conversation, no matter what the power dynamic, candidate, or hiring manager*

TRAITS CHALLENGERS SHARE WITH EXAMINERS

- *Internally focused*
- *Task focused*
- *Rely on technical skills*
- *Steadfast, inflexible*
- *Believe facts and truth matter*
- *Uncomfortable with ambiguity*
- *Uncomfortable selling themselves*
- *Don't like when the interview is surface-level; would rather ask/ answer behavioral and technical questions*
- *Could do without chitchat, don't need small talk*
- *Know how their skill set applies to the job*
- *Make a good impression by being serious and qualified*
- *Value expertise*
- *Cautious*
- *Confidence comes from intellect*

Because of this overlap, in addition to the Challenger style, there are also two variations of Challengers: Challenger/Charmer and Challenger/Examiner. Let's look a bit closer at what differentiates the three types of Charmers.

Challenger with Charmer Tendencies

A Challenger/Charmer is extroverted but less steadfast than a Challenger and Challenger/Examiner because they are more accommodating. A Challenger who shares traits with a Charmer means they are steadfast, but only to a point. They are extroverted, so interviews energize them, and they take their cues from the interviewer, but when it comes to answering interview questions about their qualifications and other technical questions, unlike Challengers, their answers do change slightly based on what they think the other person wants to hear. A Challenger with Charmer tendencies is the most flexible of Challenger styles. They are undeterred in their approach and feel as though they can persuade, convince, and cajole an interviewer by being persistent, thorough, and undaunted.

Challenger

A Challenger (without any variation) is extroverted and steadfast. Challengers are energized by other people; they open up easily and like to explain themselves. Of all the interview styles, Challengers are the most bold. They prefer unstructured interviews that feel conversational. They speak to think and have a tendency to over explain. Challengers are internally focused, and their style doesn't change depending on the situation. Challengers push boundaries, ask tough questions, and want to be seen as being truthful.

Challenger with Examiner Tendencies

The Challenger/Examiner is extroverted with introverted tendencies. They are the most restrained Challenger. They prefer to keep to themselves and put themselves out there only when they are asked to. They hold back more than Challengers and Challenger/ Charmers. They gain respect by being precise and professional. They seek attention through sharing their expertise. They have a tendency to balance out the interviewer, so if they are being interviewed by an extrovert, they may become more introverted and vice versa. Challengers with Examiner tendencies let the more dominant personality take the lead. Challenger/Examiners are specific. They ask tough questions and don't let up.

Key Takeaways

How to Tell If You Are Talking to a Challenger

- Challengers critique.

- They appraise the situation.

- They are determined.

- Challengers enjoy providing a new perspective and thoroughly examining a topic so it can be understood better.

- Challengers are not afraid to ask the tough questions.

- Interviewing is a debate or cross-examination.

- If you want a Challenger to like you, tell them you respect them and hear them.

- Challengers get you to see them as qualified by questioning.

(For practice identifying the different styles, see the Deciphering the Interview Styles activity in the Appendix.)

Strengths and Overused Strengths

Challengers have many strengths, but when they are out of balance, their intentions can be misinterpreted. The following table looks at their strengths and how those strengths can appear when they are overused.

Strengths	Overused Strengths
Strong	Inflexible
Passionate and interested	Too passionate, intense
Truthful	Tactless, undiplomatic
Determined	Arrogant
Qualified	Focus too heavily on qualifications, not enough on making a connection
Tough/Fighter	Overly aggressive, seeking something to fight against
Show their value by offering new ideas	Overly critical, unable to see the good or positive
Critic	Judgmental

Interviewing with a Challenger

I trained a group of twenty female executives in a yearlong leadership program. We met once a month and covered topics like goal setting, how to evaluate employees, and how to interview. By far the most popular session was how to interview. It was so popular they asked me to break it up into two months. One of the women was in the middle of the hiring process and found the training to be very timely. She took the interview style assessment, which revealed she was a Challenger. She agreed with the results. In our training, we went around the room and the other women shared their styles.

She confessed that she didn't agree with how most people interviewed and thought that being yourself in an interview was the best way to highlight your qualifications, skills, and abilities.

(In the same way that we all believe our style is the best one.) She was direct, no-nonsense, and committed to making a great hire. After we went around the room and she heard how her co-workers saw interviews differently, she saw that they were just as committed as she was to making a great hire and realized that perhaps her way wasn't the only way. That perhaps a charming candidate wasn't trying to get one over on her, perhaps a quiet candidate was interested, and perhaps an accommodating person did know what they wanted.

In my interview training I teach clients to write down what they want ahead of time and tell it to an accountability partner, preferably someone who will co-interview with them. All too often we change our mind in the hiring process when we meet candidates: "Well, I thought I wanted someone with those skills, but now I want what this person is offering." Or our bias gets in the way when we misinterpret styles that we don't understand.

She spent the next month interviewing for her open position and, relying on our training, questioned why she liked the candidates she did.

When we met the next month to do the second part of our interview training, she raised her hand and said, "As you know, I am in the middle of hiring for a role in my department, and I used the techniques that we went over last month. Denise is my accountability partner and I told her what we needed in the role and she co-interviewed with me. In the interviews, there was a clear favorite for me. I liked the first candidate so much because he answered questions directly. The second candidate drove me crazy in the interview. He took too long to answer questions, he paused, and he was contemplative. After the interview in our debrief I confided this to Denise. She pushed back and made me see that the second candidate has the right qualities for the role. As much as I didn't want to admit it, she was right. I did need those qualities in this role, but it was hard to see that when I felt a connection more strongly with the other candidate. So instead I hired the one who bothered me in the interview. He started last week, and so far he's been the best hire I have ever made."

Just like this story, a lot of Challengers find it hard to connect with other styles. A lot of hiring managers get into trouble when they continually hire people who are like them. I tell them, "We don't need another you; we have you, we need someone different." But it is very hard to see past our own style, to accept that when others do it differently, that can also be right. To interview better means to take into account other people's styles and differences.

Why Challengers Need to Be Heard

One of our deepest longings is that other people should acknowledge our feelings, understand our suffering, and notice our anxieties. Challengers embody this. They make an impression by putting themselves out there so it can be acknowledged. They need to be heard.

A Challenger becomes more challenging when they aren't being validated or listened to. Perhaps they were never listened to when it mattered. Their need to challenge comes from a fear that they won't be heard, that their viewpoint is irrelevant, and they are not good enough.

Because of their need to be heard, a Challenger can diminish others by being too stubborn and insisting on their version of the story, dismissing other's opinions and views. They instinctually disagree with others because they think it is the best way to show that they are qualified. They see challenging everything as a value add in the same way a Charmer sees being likable as a value add. A Challenger, therefore, can't always hear other people because they don't make it a point to listen.

How Challengers Can Manage Their Need to Be Heard

Challengers are not alone for wanting to be understood. We are far less inclined to need to be heard when we are acknowledged—feelings ease when they've been given an airing. Find someone you trust, someone you can be vulnerable with to practice your approach. Get an outside perspective on the impression you are making. You won't need to be validated in an interview if you have already talked it out with someone.

Practice a mock interview and prepare how to talk about yourself so you don't drone on and on. Practice acknowledging that other people's opinions are valuable too, and that you are not the only one who wants to be heard or who has a story to tell.

Recognize that others have a need to be heard, and your need is not any greater than theirs. Your approach can be unfair to them. In the way that a Charmer/Harmonizer is unfair to themselves by putting themselves last, you are unfair to others by putting yourself first.

Delivering bad news with frankness, being too straightforward with tough questions, or giving feedback in a curt way feels uncaring to others. Learn that there is a time and place to insist on your viewpoint; choose your battles.

Instead of banging a fist on the table and insisting on your point, recognize that there are moments when it is best to sidestep conflict, that not all battles need to be waged and there are times when lessons can't be learned. Challengers would benefit from recognizing that timing and priorities matter when it comes to what point you want to make. Wait and be strategic so your points have the best chance of being heard.

Challengers also need to learn to listen. Encourage other people when they tell a story. Be curious. Ask questions that pertain to the story they are telling. Refer back to something someone has said previously or earlier in the interview. Be receptive rather than assuming the worst, or investigating. Not everyone is hiding something. Go in with a goal to clarify underlying issues, not make your own point. Go in wanting to get to the heart of the matter, not prove yourself. Listening well means putting aside your own agenda and ego. Active listening requires active body language, occasional *hmm*s and head nods. Active listening requires that you make eye contact, pay attention. You don't moralize or pass judgment but are interested and ask questions out of curiosity, not questions that lead to the point you hope to make when it's your turn to talk. Listening requires that you go off what the other person is saying, not just reporting or saying what you want to say.

 INTERVIEW PRINCIPLE FOR JOB SEEKERS

Active listening is key to showing your interviewer you are engaged. Make eye contact as they speak, nod your head, and make occasional agreeing sounds.

Put yourself in the shoes of the other person or imagine the great pleasure of being listened to. To interview better, Challengers need to balance their need to be heard with an ability to listen.

Challengers can recognize that everyone has a need to be heard. Remember that people may disagree with you and that's okay. If you are not feeling heard, it may not be about you. You don't need others to agree with you or even listen to you to know that you are valuable and worthy. You can give that to yourself.

When Challengers Interview Well

Challengers can be insightful and direct. They are often undaunted in their approach. They are self-possessed and don't worry about ruffling a few feathers. They get to the bottom of things and right to the heart of the matter. They are often described as "radically honest and totally transparent." They ask questions, not because they want to get to know you but because they have internal requirements that they need to meet, questions they need answered. A Challenger who interviews well knows what those requirements are, and communicates so as to not make the other person defensive. They may or may not tell you what those internal requirements are.

A Challenger who interviews well balances the diplomacy of a Charmer and the need to fit in like a Harmonizer. They check in with their audience, reassure them, and make affirmations. They listen first then ask the tough questions. They balance their need to be heard with the needs of others. To interview better, they may feel like they are holding themselves back, but this restraint is not inauthentic but respectful. Authenticity is not about being unfiltered, it's not saying whatever comes to mind. It's about integrity; staying true to yourself doesn't mean voicing every opinion, just the ones that matter to you.

When Challengers Interview Poorly

When a Challenger interviews poorly, it's often because they are overly relying on their ability to investigate and question. They may come off as too critical or judgmental. They lack the self-awareness to realize that they are isolating their audience by insisting on asking a million questions. While they believe their constant questions help them arrive at their own conclusions and form opinions, the other person can feel annoyed, suffocated, or, worse, harassed.

I was in a meeting once with a Challenger, and he was very nice and very passionate and even complimentary, but his style of asking question after question left me feeling exhausted. He was too intense, too demanding.

Since they are undaunted, they have a tendency to bring up topics or have conversations that might be inappropriate for that phase of the interview, like asking an entry-level recruiter on a phone screen, "I read about the recent corporate issues; what's your five-year plan to right the ship?" A question like this one would make a better impression if saved for a final-round interview, because an executive is better poised to answer it and have a conversation about it. Of all the interview styles, Challengers have a very hard time changing up their style depending on who they are interviewing with. There is a time and place for certain questions. Put it this way: it's unlikely that an entry-level recruiter is going to pass someone on to the next round if they ask that question. You may be seen as combative and contentious. Instead, save it for the right person.

 INTERVIEW PRINCIPLE FOR JOB SEEKERS

Ask the right people the right questions. Ask HR people questions about company culture and next steps in the interview process. Save questions about the job and where it will lead for the hiring manager.

Challengers have a tendency to talk through their thinking. When they interview poorly, they talk too much, are long-winded, and lose their audience. It's best if Challengers do their thinking before the interview so they are prepared with concise, clear answers.

How to Interview a Challenger Job Seeker

An interview is a strange artificial experience, where someone has something that you want—a job or a promotion—and the hiring manager is in a position of power. This dynamic doesn't bring out the best in Challengers. A Challenger would rather be the one asking the questions, so interviewing a Challenger can feel like the power dynamic is off.

The conversational push and pull can feel almost argumentative, and since Challengers are highly skeptical you will feel as if they doubt most of what you say.

Remember that Challengers see skepticism and doubt as a value add. They offer their opinions, critiques, and judgments as ways to provide a new perspective because they ultimately want to get to the heart of the matter or figure it out. To a Challenger, having a tough conversation is the only way to see if you can work together. They don't see confrontation as a negative, rather as an imperative. The need to test the relationship, to check the legitimacy of someone's claims to see if the job is a good fit.

When a Challenger doesn't feel heard, they get more argumentative and push harder to win their case. To satiate them, tell them you hear them and that you appreciate their perspective. If you refuse to acknowledge them, they will continue and not feel like you understood.

How to Interview with a Challenger Hiring Manager

There is a bias toward Challengers as hiring managers because they are natural questioners, so there is a belief that their style makes them great interviewers. It can also make them hard to interview with.

I worked with a Challenger once who told me that if a candidate doesn't answer the behavioral questions in a particular way, he would not pass them on to the next round. Since Challengers prioritize the truth, they bristle at stories or answers that are not based around work. They want the answers to be a certain way, which is incredibly unfair to candidates, because how is a candidate supposed to know what the "right" answer is? It's not possible.

Challenger hiring mangers are intense. They believe that an interview is the time to get to the bottom of a person's qualifications. Often the interview may feel like a cross-examination or interrogation. I went to a superday interview (an all day interview event) for an organization that was recruiting a bunch of interns. Often these begin with a breakfast, a little networking with partners, and then each candidate was sent off to meet with hiring managers one by one until lunch. When I walked in, I noticed a hiring manager engaging in small talk with a prospective intern: "What do you do for fun?" The intern said he loved to play tennis and go to the beach. Instead of having the conversation become a back-and-forth, the hiring manager didn't reciprocate by offering what they did for fun, instead just asking another question: "Where do you go to the beach?" The candidate answered, and so the one-sided conversation went. When a Challenger is getting their needs met, they are getting all their questions answered, but this style doesn't lead to a connection or intimacy. It feels to the candidate like they were just interrogated.

Know that Challengers' questioning technique is not a reflection of you, but how they conduct every interview. Don't let the many questions overwhelm you; if you have practiced sufficiently and developed your self-awareness, these questions should be easy—they are about you!

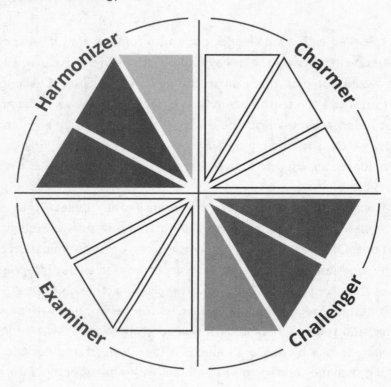

How a Challenger Interviews with Their Opposite—the Harmonizer

Harmonizers rely on their ability to read the other person, to connect with them, and look for ways they can adapt accordingly. Unlike Challengers, who are task focused, expressive, and don't change their interview style depending on the situation, Harmonizers will defer to the other person to determine who will lead the conversation. Challengers are comfortable in this dynamic because Challengers easily take the lead. Harmonizers will take an interest in who you are, leaving you feeling that they wanted to get to know you, rather than selling the job or talking about your skills or your interest in the job. Don't take their interest in you as a person as disinterest in you working for them. Harmonizers have a more social and low-key approach, whereas Challengers are all business. They will not make the focused impression Challengers pride themselves on, but they will make people feel heard, and feeling heard and respected is a priority for a Challenger, so the conversation will feel natural to both of you.

How You Can Balance Your Approach and Tap into the Other Styles

Challengers can be more successful if they pull traits from other styles to balance out their natural tendencies:

- *Challengers can soften their approach by flexing their style the way a Charmer does.*
- *Challengers can tap into the reserved nature of Examiners and strive to hold some things back.*
- *Challengers can learn more about their audience if they employ Harmonizer tendencies and ask more questions about how they would fit into the culture as opposed to telling people how they will fit in.*

Advice for Challengers

Pre-interview Mantras for Challengers to Manage Their Need to Be Heard

It pays to trust.

""I am worthy and valuable."

"I don't need to say everything to be heard."

Key Takeaways for Challenger Job Seekers

- You are not afraid to bring up tough subjects, but this can backfire and isolate your audience. Do not ask tough questions before you have built rapport. There's a time and place for those questions; pace yourself.

- Remember, it's not your job to lead the interview. Learn to be led. Let the interviewer ask you questions and trust that your whole story and who you are will shine through over time. You don't have to tell them everything in the first five minutes.

Key Takeaways for Challenger Hiring Managers

- Just because your job as an interviewer is to ask questions (your specialty) doesn't mean you can just barrage the candidate.

- Watch your intensity and number of questions. Remember this is not an interrogation or cross-examination. An interview conducted well is a two-way street. Allow time for the candidate to ask you questions as well.

- Get comfortable with ambiguity.

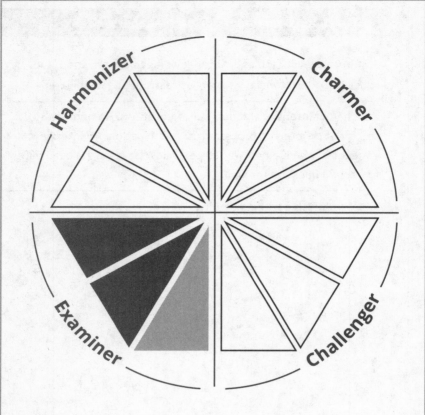

Examiner. Reserved in interviews, they are focused internally and are not especially interested in seeking approval. Others may describe them as quiet and hesitating. They come across as serious. Their interview answers display their mastery of the process, facts, and details. They might have been given feedback that they are too quiet. They are not interested in charming the interviewer. They prioritize facts and expertise, not what makes a good impression. Overall, they believe getting hired should be a direct result of being good at the job, not being good at interviewing. They would rather take a test to get hired for a job than have an interview.

Examiner

"I want to get it right."

I had an initial conversation with a prospective new client who came to me because he kept getting passed over for jobs that he interviewed for. He told me that interviewing is like acting and he hated it. "I refuse to network or sell myself," he said, accentuating "sell myself" with air quotes. I was intrigued by his disgust. I asked him if he was unwilling to sell himself, then who did he expect would sell him? He was happy I asked: "I don't think pretending to be happy and upbeat should be a requirement to get a job. That shouldn't be the way to sell myself. I'd rather talk about my qualifications to prove that I am a good fit than engage in small talk." I agreed. "Often, we interview people using the wrong system to determine talent; we are almost always conducting a social interview. I think what you are onto is, why are recruiters basing their decisions to hire you on your ability to have a conversation, not your technical skills, right?"

INTERVIEW PRINCIPLE FOR HIRING MANAGERS

Often, we conduct social interviews, which are closer to conversations. Behavioral interviews can decrease ambiguity, and are more effective and less biased.

When I was the director of talent, I saw this approach play out many times. The candidates came across as closed off and disinterested. I didn't think about it any further than that. I passed on them, moved them to the do-not-call pile, and went on with my day. But after coaching thousands of clients, I saw that this candidate's approach was a distinct style, and while it was the opposite of my own approach as a Charmer, it had its own merits. I saw that he wanted to make a good impression the same way I did. He just went about it a different way.

I told him that we could create a strategy that would allow him to "sell himself" in a way that felt authentic. He was skeptical.

I explained that recruiters, HR folks, and hiring managers aren't just looking to see if you can do the job technically, they are also trying to figure out if they want to work with you every day. Even though you might check all the technical boxes, and they know you can do the job, they also need to feel like you will be the right culture fit. That means they need to know who you are, and your attitude, so they can assess how you will fit into the team. Aside from being able to articulate why you're the best candidate for the job, hiring managers are looking for someone they like. Likeability is an important factor that shouldn't be discounted. Examiners need to be seen as qualified; they don't prioritize likeability. Instead of being pushed to "act" like Charmers, Examiners can shift their approach to better accommodate the need for likeability, while still remaining true to themselves.

Something that Examiners don't always realize is that in order to interview better you need to use a different skill set than the one you might need to do the job. You need to use emotional intelligence. In Daniel Goleman's groundbreaking book *Emotional Intelligence*, he writes, "People who make an excellent social impression, for example, are adept at monitoring their own expression of emotion, are keenly attuned to the ways others are reacting, and so are able to continually fine-tune their social performance, adjusting it to make sure they are having the desired effect. In that sense, they are like skilled actors." While adapting your approach based on feedback you gather from the other person is something that Charmers are great at, it's often a challenge for Examiners because it feels inauthentic.

My client was on to something; he probably had seen a few of his less qualified friends get jobs purely on their "acting abilities." Some people are so adept at making an impression or getting people to like them that they become what Goleman calls "social chameleons, who don't mind saying one thing and doing another if it will win them social approval," i.e., getting the job. And that does happen all too often, leaving many like my client annoyed and distrustful of the hiring process. Which, in turn, affected his performance in interviews.

I encouraged my client to use his emotional intelligence to stay true to himself without isolating his audience. Interviewing, I told him, isn't about telling someone what they want to hear, because, truthfully, you have no idea what someone wants to hear. It's about highlighting the best version of you in the most authentic way possible. Goleman goes on to say, "If these interpersonal abilities are not balanced by an astute sense of one's own needs and feelings and how to fulfill them, they can lead to a hollow social success—a popularity won at the cost of one's true satisfaction." This is a key point I discussed in chapter 5; authenticity is essential because without it you might find yourself in a role that isn't right for you.

There is hope for my Examiner client who is stubborn and would rather risk coming across as a jerk or disinterested than a "social chameleon" because he already has the capacity to be "true to himself, which allows acting in accord with one's deepest feelings and values no matter what the social consequence." Such emotional integrity will lead him to landing the right job because he will be unwilling to settle for something that isn't in line with what he wants, but in order to get what he wants he must soften his edges and use his emotional intelligence.

Examiners See Interviews as a Test

In a corporate training seminar, I told the story of how a Charmer in a previous training said, "When I go home after an interview and my husband asks me how it went, I say, 'Good, they liked me.'" An Examiner then raised his hand and said, "I am thinking about how I would describe an interview to my wife. For me, I don't think about if someone likes me, I think a lot about my answers to questions and worry and stress over how I did, if I got it right."

I saw this play out in mock interviews with clients and students who were Examiners. Examiner after Examiner would come prepared for the interview by having memorized their answers. It was like listening to someone read off a script. Their answers were just enough; they wouldn't elaborate or give too many details. They were solely focused on answering the question. They would overlook body language, their presence, and how they made someone feel. To Examiners, an interview is about their qualifications, nothing more, and their interview style reflects that. Examiners see interviews as pass or fail. They will get it right or wrong.

An Examiner client told me once that he didn't want to learn how to interview because he didn't want it to be about his interview skills. He just wanted to show them why he was qualified. The "other stuff" felt weird to him. For me, a Charmer who prioritizes the other stuff, I thought his perspective was interesting. I proposed that maybe neither one of us was right, and perhaps the best approach would be a combination of our two styles. Where Charmers need to add more details and metrics and substance to their answers, Examiners need to open up, add some of their personality, and connect more.

Steve

Steve, an Examiner, came to me years ago. He was a firefighter and was coming up on a big promotional interview. Firefighter promotions are based on three things: seniority, a test, and an interview. He had already nailed the test and now he needed to nail the interview. But he was anxious because he went up for the same promotion four years before and bombed the interview. He told me the stakes were high and it was his to lose, and he didn't want to lose it again.

He became a firefighter right after school, and his last interview was to get into the academy. It had been over twenty years since then, and he lamented that he was never taught to interview, yet his future depended on it. This was his last shot at a promotion before he retired. A lot was riding on this interview; his pension would be set on this next position. It made him very motivated. He was a great student, and he was also quite hard on himself. It was tough for him to let anything go. He really wanted to have a script and be perfect, and I had to remind him that that wasn't how it worked, and with enough practice he wouldn't feel like he needed to rely on a script.

Examiners are introverted; they don't open up easily. Introverts think to speak, which means they need time to formulate their ideas. They need time after you ask them a question to think a bit before answering. For Steve, going into an interview was daunting. I told him the way to feel more confident was to be more prepared. We worked on his interview answers, and he practiced by recording his answers and playing them back so he could critique himself and ask for my feedback. He took his interview prep seriously, and I loved coaching him.

Examiners are also private; they do not like opening up to a stranger. An interview feels like an unnatural setting to them. They prefer to keep their emotions and feelings to themselves.

Steve told me that he thought he'd bombed the previous interview because he didn't open up; he thought he was just bad at interviews. He said he felt too stiff and didn't feel comfortable explaining why he was a good fit. Mainly, he was disappointed that he'd sold himself short.

In one of our sessions, Steve said, "I need to tell you something," in a tone that sounded like he was going to say something awful. I prepared myself for the worst, and then Steve let me in on a secret: a long time ago, he had wanted to be a comedian, and he'd done some stand-up comedy. He thought this might help with interviews.

I agreed. Examiners aren't generally comfortable being the star of the show, so I was pleasantly surprised that he had spent some time on a stage. Charmers and Challengers are usually the ones more comfortable in the spotlight and putting themselves out there. I said, "Sounds like there's a showman in there. Let's tap into that. Think about this interview as part performance and part test."

I knew he was hesitant to make anything personal or really bring himself to the interview, so I encouraged him over and over to show himself a bit more, to be more of himself. Knowing yourself and being yourself come across as confident in the interview.

After one of our sessions, he texted me that he'd gotten out his old VHS tapes of his stand-up comedy performances and watched them to get inspired. He'd then set up a camera in his basement and recorded himself answering interview questions. Part test. Part performance. He would bring clips to our sessions to show me, and he recorded our sessions so he could take notes. He devised his own way to get comfortable with being himself and nailing the answers.

 INTERVIEW PRINCIPLE FOR JOB SEEKERS

Record yourself as you practice answering interview questions. Seeing yourself from another perspective can help show you where you have room for improvement.

In every session, Steve always said, "I am just not good at interviews." And I always said, "That's not true; you had *one* bad interview, that doesn't mean you aren't good at interviews." It's normal to dwell on interviews we didn't do our best in, but Steve was overly critical about his past performance. This might have been because Examiners are so focused on getting it right, so when they don't, they feel as though they have failed.

 INTERVIEW PRINCIPLE FOR JOB SEEKERS

You aren't bad at interviewing; you are just unprepared.

For lots of emergency service employees like Steve—for example, firemen and police officers—interviews can be especially nerve-racking because they are generally done by a panel of three to five people. Other industries conduct panel interviews as well, like academia and government. Unlike the corporate world, where there are two to four interviews and several opportunities in different settings (from the phone screen to a one-on-one interview), first responders often only have one shot: the panel interview. And if that isn't stressful enough, you also know who your competition is because the process is public. For Steve, he was up against three other guys. He had the most seniority (which is a very important factor), but the other two guys had more experience interviewing, and they were younger.

It is especially hard to not think about your competition during the interview process. Some clients fall into the trap of obsessing about what the other candidates can offer, what they are going to do and say, and how they compare. They drive themselves crazy about the imagined person. It's even harder when you know who you're going up against. Some corporations interview a lot of internal candidates, and you may hear through the grapevine who you're up against—could be a coworker, or worse, a subordinate. When this happens, I have seen clients lose focus on themselves and create interview answers to contradict their imagined competition, to pit themselves against the other person. They think it's strategic, but it's not. It's a lot of guesswork to imagine what your competition might say and those assumptions are often not accurate. I encourage my clients to use their energy on crafting great authentic answers and controlling only what they can control: themselves.

For Steve, our last hurdle in boosting his confidence was me encouraging him to ignore the competition and trust himself. The day before the big interview, I said to him, "If you're running a marathon, you don't waste your limited and precious energy on looking behind you to see where the competition is, do you? You keep your head down and you focus on your training; you focus on the finish line in front of you, not what's behind you. An interview is the same: don't waste energy thinking about the other candidates you are up against."

 INTERVIEW PRINCIPLE FOR JOB SEEKERS

It isn't helpful to spend time focusing on your competition. There's no way to prove that your assumptions about them are correct, and you waste precious time thinking about others when you should be building your own self-awareness. Your best bet is not to know your competition, but to know yourself and be able to convey clearly who you are.

The big day of the interview came. Of the three candidates, he was the last to interview. His interview was at two p.m. After the interview, he texted me, "All done. I felt good, I did my best, better than before, and this time even if I don't get the promotion, I made myself proud."

I was also proud of him. In our work together, Steve learned how to open up. He learned how to prepare great stories that he infused with his personality and reasoning of why he was qualified. He learned to focus on himself, not the competition. But most importantly, he learned having one bad interview doesn't mean you're bad at interviews.

I got a text from him a few days after the interview—he got the promotion!

Approach and Style

Focused on the details, the technicalities, and the task at hand, Examiners prioritize being knowledgeable. Examiners are steadfast and often make a serious impression. Their interview answers display their mastery of the process, facts, and details. They want to be seen as qualified. Examiners highlight their analytical and logical skills so they will be seen as competent, but they downplay their other qualities. They want to give verifiable answers that are consistent and accurate rather than stories that entertain.

The need to get it right drives them to be precise, but it can also drive them to leave out the human element of the story, to downplay their humanity. They may come across as singularly focused and inflexible. That rigidity can work against them. In the way that their polar opposite, the Charmer, prioritizes being accommodating and may come across as disingenuous, an Examiner may make a one-dimensional impression, only talking about the job and their skills. They can come across as robotic. Interviewers may report that they didn't really feel like they got to know them.

A critical element for an Examiner to work on is accepting that the interviewer wants to get to know you; they want to know who you are and what you're like because they are assessing not only your ability to do the job but also if they want to work with you. Will you be a good fit on the team? Examiners have a tendency to downplay and even ignore this part of the interview, dismissing it as not relevant or not a valuable part of the process.

Examiners are introverted and private. As introverts they require time to think before they speak. They speak more slowly than extroverts, and their answers are more thoughtful, and they sound less nervous than a fast-paced extrovert. Examiners need more time in an interview. Short screening interviews are especially challenging for an Examiner since they don't open up quickly and the pressure of a ten-minute phone screening can make them shut down. If you want to get an Examiner to open up, take it slow, schedule enough time with them, and don't ask probing questions at the beginning. They are slow to warm. They will open up, but not in the first five minutes.

 INTERVIEW PRINCIPLE FOR JOB SEEKERS

Taking time to answer makes a better impression; you come across as thoughtful as opposed to rushing and talking fast.

Think of every introvert that you know: How many of them like small talk? How many of them like to share details about themselves to a perfect stranger, especially when there is a job on the line?

I had a client who was very, very quiet. Interviewing him was painful. I felt bad that I was asking him so many questions because I knew he did not want to answer them. His answers were at most thirty to forty-five seconds long. They were direct, specific, and factual: "Why'd you major in Actuarial Science?" "I've always been good at math." Generally, recruiters and hiring managers ask an interview question like this to get the candidate to open up, to get the conversation going. His answer didn't give me a lot to go on, but I persisted, "Is the Actuarial Program living up to your expectations? Do you like living in Philadelphia?" "Yes." Once I realized all I was getting was a one-word answer, I made a nonverbal cue for him to go on, and he got flustered and added more to his answer: "I enjoy it here."

Examiners have a tendency to want to fast-forward through small talk. They want to get to the real interview questions, but, like I told this client and all the Examiners I work with, small talk isn't just part of the interview—in some unstructured interviews, those

without predetermined questions, small talk can be the whole interview. Your interviewer, especially if they are a Charmer, may
never ask you traditional interview questions, so you need to be
prepared to talk about yourself and sell yourself conversationally.

Examiners have a hard time talking about anything that isn't directly related to the job, the company, or their qualifications. They
believe a job should be won by the most qualified candidate, not
the candidate who interviews the best. But jobs are won all the time
by people who interview well. Examiners are passed over in favor of
a candidate who put themselves out there.

Examiners are often very focused on answering questions from
a technical perspective. Since they look at an interview like a test,
their answers tend to be verifiable, factual answers rather than
stories. But people are more likely to remember a story that you
tell as opposed to reciting your resume. This can be hard for Examiners as storytelling isn't their strong suit. Many interviews are
based on behavioral interview techniques, and many interviewers rely on asking behavioral questions like, "Tell me about a time
you dealt with a tough client." The answer to a question like this
can't be just a few cut-and-dried sentences. It requires a story
for a response, and the ideal answer is one that uses the STAR
method (see Chapter 6 for more on this method). Practicing
STAR responses can help an Examiner move past their difficulty
being vulnerable. It can help teach them that there is a place for
storytelling in an interview.

Examiners also prepare for interviews by deciding on their answers ahead of time. Because the answers are the way to "get it
right." Once in an interview, they do not deviate from their script.
If an interviewer asks a follow-up question or asks them to elaborate, they may get flustered. If an Examiner gets the sense that
the interview isn't going well or that the interviewer doesn't like
them, their attitude may be affected, but they will not change their

answers. Whereas a Charmer or Harmonizer will change course immediately and change their position and attitude to appease the interviewer, Challengers and Examiners do not. They are steadfast in their approach; they don't waffle, they don't bend, and they certainly don't tell tall tales.

Examiners assume the interviewer will mistake enthusiasm for insincerity, so they tend to rely on being impartial, serious, and all about the technicalities. An interviewer may see their "all business" attitude as too rigid or too inflexible. That being said, it's hard not to appreciate an Examiner in an interview. They are dedicated to making a good impression. Their value to an organization is obvious. They are detailed, specific, undaunted, and inquisitive.

I interviewed a candidate for a sales role, and he was an Examiner. There's a stereotype that salespeople should be Charmers (highly extroverted and accommodating), so he was a breath of fresh air. He said his sales philosophy was to be in the background and let the client take center stage. He said that his most powerful sales tactic was to listen. I thought he was very well qualified and passed him on to meet with our EVP of sales (a Charmer). When we debriefed after the interview, the EVP dismissed him as too passive, too submissive. I thought it was a big mistake, so I pushed back and told him that not every salesperson is aggressive. I wasn't able to convince him to give him a shot. But our competitor did, and he went on to be very successful. A lesson and a big loss for us.

That lesson stayed with me. So did the lessons I've learned from all my introverted clients and students.

In Michaela Chung's book *The Irresistible Introvert*, she describes introversion not as a liability but as a special skill: "One third to one half of Americans are introverts in a culture that celebrates—even enforces—an ideal of extroversion and a cult of personality." Chung asserts that introverts are just as powerful in their unique ways.

I knew that the EVP was not a quiet minority and that most people can't see the "irresistible charm" of introverts, as Chung puts it. To become a better coach and teacher, I wanted to better understand what makes an introvert tick so I could help them sell themselves in a way that was unapologetic and authentic to their introverted nature. Chung argues that because society tends to have a bias for extroverts, "A lot of introverts waste time trying on every style of extroverted charisma, cramming ourselves into personas that are entirely the wrong shape and size for us." After working with so many introverts, I can see the value of their approach, and that they don't need to change who they are to be successful.

Just because introverts are quiet doesn't mean they don't have anything to say. Just because they have a different style doesn't mean it's wrong. In all my years coaching introverted clients, I've found the best way to encourage them to open up is to meet them where they are. Extroverts, like myself, have a tendency to say things like, "Just open up," "Talk more," or "Why are you so quiet?" As Chung goes on to say, "Introverts have been chastised for our tight-lipped ways. Extroverts love to point out how quiet we are. You've probably been asked, 'Why are you so quiet?' several times in your life. And I bet it hasn't once made you want to launch into a soliloquy about why you don't talk much." More helpful advice is to be specific about what more introverts should say. Again, the STAR method is incredibly helpful as a template for creating stories that adequately paint a picture but don't feel too excessive.

I worked with a president of an organization who was highly introverted and the number one salesperson at the company. When I found that out, to be very honest, I was shocked because he was so quiet, so humble. Then it dawned on me: he is a great listener, he gets prospects to open up, and he pulls them in with a quiet contemplation that is disarming. As the subtitle of Chung's book says,

"Harness the power of quiet charisma in a loud world," and he did that in spades.

At their best, an Examiner balances their need to get it right with warmth and curiosity. They know that small talk can provide important insight and information about the other person that will ultimately help them do well in the interview. For introverts, small talk provides a nice warm-up to the intimacy of an interview. It gives them ways to connect and gives them the space to find the courage to reveal who they are. A study in reciprocity shows us that when we confide in someone, they themselves confide something in us. Small talk is the shallow end of the pool of conversational intimacy. There is beauty and complexity and subtlety in common, mundane small-talk subjects like the weather, traffic, and popular culture, but you won't see the complexity if you have a closed mind. Be open-minded, and people may surprise you. Being a good conversationalist is not a talent that should be diminished. Being open-minded and a good listener means that you pick up on the attitudes of your new boss when they talk about their commute in. When your prospective coworker tells you about the issues that the company has overcome and the receptionist babbles on about competitors, you might see opportunities for growth at the company.

People often fear small talk because they think they won't be able to steer a conversation and will become the victims of others' petty interests. But Examiners are good listeners and will pick up on interesting themes in a conversation. They do not feel compelled in the way Charmers do to just offer up their own similar stories (let me double down on your story of your flat tire on your way in to work by telling you about the time that happened to me), but they ask profound questions and know that no matter what anyone is talking about they will learn something, because they are always looking to learn something. Examiners are very sincere. And sincerity is the heart of a good conversation.

From left to right: Examiner with Challenger tendencies, Examiner, and Examiner with Harmonizer tendencies

Examiner Variations

Like all interview styles, there is variation within the Examiner style. As you can see in the interview style hexagon, Examiners are closest to Challengers and Harmonizers, and often share traits with these styles.

TRAITS EXAMINERS SHARE WITH CHALLENGERS

- *Internally focused*
- *Task focused*
- *Rely on technical skills*
- *Steadfast, inflexible*
- *Believe facts and truth matter*
- *Uncomfortable with ambiguity*
- *Uncomfortable selling themselves*
- *Don't like when the interview is surface-level; would rather ask/answer behavioral and technical questions*
- *Could do without chitchat, don't need small talk*
- *Know how their skill set applies to the job*

- *Make a good impression by being serious and qualified*
- *Value expertise*
- *Cautious*
- *Precise*
- *Confidence comes from intellect*

TRAITS EXAMINERS SHARE WITH HARMONIZERS

- *Reserved*
- *Not going to volunteer something that is not on their resume*
- *Introverted; provide limited access to just their public persona and work life*
- *Slow to warm*
- *Think to speak*
- *Quiet*
- *Answers are short and to the point*
- *Don't lead conversations*
- *Solve problems by thinking them through*

Because of this overlap, in addition to the Examiner style, there are also two variations of Examiners: Examiner/Challenger and Examiner/Harmonizer. Let's look a bit closer at what differentiates the three types of Examiners.

Examiner with Challenger Tendencies

Examiner/Challengers are introverted with extroverted tendencies. They are the most outgoing Examiner. They are naturally inclined to be reserved but "turn it on" in an interview setting.

They prefer to keep to themselves but are willing to put themselves out there more than the other Examiner styles. They talk and share more than Examiners and Examiner/Harmonizers. They gain respect by being precise and professional. They seek attention through sharing their expertise. They have a tendency to balance out the interviewer, so if they are being interviewed by an extrovert they may become more introverted and vice versa. Examiners with Challenger tendencies let the more dominant personality take the lead. Examiner/Challengers are specific; they answer interview questions in very detailed and precise ways. They pick their battles and are cautious in interviews.

Examiner

An Examiner (without any variation) is introverted and steadfast. An interview is not a natural setting for an introvert because they are not generally ready to open up to someone within a few minutes of meeting them. They are private and keep their emotions and enthusiasm to themselves. They play it close to the vest. Of all the interview styles, Examiners are the most straightforward. They prefer structured, one-on-one interviews. Because they think to speak, Examiners need time to collect themselves and prepare their thoughts and answers before answering tough questions. Since they are more quiet than the other styles, they often ask more insightful questions, and are generally more thoughtful and better listeners.

Examiners are internally focused, always thinking about their answers. Their style doesn't change depending on the interviewer's feedback. Neither a positive nor negative response from an interviewer elicits a change in their style. Examiners are consistent. They make a good impression by "getting it right."

Examiner with Harmonizer Tendencies

Examiner/Harmonizers are steadfast with accommodating tendencies. They are the most willing to adapt of any of the Examiners. They hold back until something piques their interest and will get involved in a conversation only if the topic interests them. They are more likely to observe the conversation if others are talking. They do not steer the conversation to them or change the subject. Their conversational style is about others; they do not talk about themselves or share details that are personal. They are private, quiet, and unassuming. Examiners with Harmonizer tendencies never take the lead.

How to Tell If You Are Talking to an Examiner

- Examiners are quiet and they listen.

- They are private.

- Examiners enjoy giving answers that are factual and reliable.

- They come across as private and trusted.

- They are not afraid to give the unpopular opinion if it means being right.

- They are not afraid to be seen as serious, no-nonsense, and all business.

- Examiners get you to see them as qualified by being precise.

(For practice identifying the different styles, see the Deciphering the Interview Styles activity in the Appendix.)

Strengths and Overused Strengths

Examiners have many strengths, but when they are out of balance, their intentions can be misinterpreted. The following table looks at their strengths and how those strengths can appear when they are overused.

Strengths	Overused Strengths
Serious	Unsure or uninterested
Professional or all business	Their answers can be one-dimensional, all about work.
Precise and facts-based	Their answers are very short and only give the facts.
Impartial, not interested in getting someone to like them	Aloof or cold
Qualified	Focus too heavily on their qualifications, not enough on making a connection
Perfectionist	Overly particular, look for mistakes, focus on the negative, and can't accept things as they are
Knowledgeable	Overly critical. Dark side of that is they may never be able to see the good or positive. Everything is critiqued.
Analytical/Logical	Downplay their more fun qualities and don't show their personal side

10

Interviewing with an Examiner

In 2011, my first year teaching college students, I met Rasheed, a freshman. He was a good kid, always cheerful and enthusiastic. He was also disorganized. Usually dressed in the most wrinkled T-shirt and ill-matched shorts, with shoes that were inappropriate for the season. I met with him one-on-one to edit and rewrite his resume. He dug his resume out of the bottom of his backpack. His resume was the paper version of his wrinkled T-shirt. He scrambled to find a pencil. His work experience was lacking, his thoughts were scattered, and he was unsure about what to put on his resume. After talking for twenty minutes, I found out that he waited tables throughout high school at a family friend's high-end Indian restaurant, and he explained how it taught him how to be professional and multitask. As someone who'd waited tables myself, I could relate. He had been resistant to write about his restaurant job on his resume because he thought that it didn't matter, that it wasn't transferable, and it was "just waiting tables." He was a risk management major, and he told me that he just figured that restaurant work didn't have anything to do with being in insurance. I explained to him that all jobs are valuable and shared with him my experience working in restaurants. I helped him rewrite his resume to be a better representation of his skills. By the time he left our resume review, he had a new appreciation for his work experience and a well-written resume. But as he walked out of the room, I thought, *That kid is not going anywhere.*

 INTERVIEW PRINCIPLE FOR JOB SEEKERS

All jobs are valuable, and you will be more confident when you look at your experience without criticism. Updating your resume is a good exercise to building an appreciation for your past roles. If you can reflect objectively on your experience, you can reflect on all that you've done and begin to make connections to where you're hoping to go.

When I started teaching, I had come right out of the corporate world, and I was cocky. I had just spent a decade interviewing and recruiting people, and I thought I had "the instinct." So when I met Rasheed, I used the recruiting sixth sense that I had relied on all those years before to judge him. I concluded that he was a nice kid, but he wasn't going to get an internship. But the great thing about teaching at a college for a decade is that I get to know so many students, year after year, during a period in their lives when they change so much. When they grow into themselves and find themselves.

The next year, when he was a sophomore, I taught him again, and I noticed that he was more mature, more relaxed, more sure of himself. I remember noticing this, but it did not change my opinion of him. When he was a junior, I was in my third year of teaching and coaching. I had seen enough clients and met enough students that I was losing my cocky instinct. I was starting to see people in a new way. When Rasheed came back as a junior, he had matured; gone were the wrinkly T-shirts and half-assed resume. I had matured as well. I no longer relied on my initial impressions to make judgments of people. I was more open; I started to see the whole person.

Rasheed had taken his summer seriously and in addition to waiting tables, he'd gotten an internship at a family friend's company, and he was committed to getting a "real internship." The following spring, he landed one of the most competitive and coveted internships in our program.

When he returned as a senior for his last resume review with me in October, he had already received three job offers. He was over the moon, and I was happy for him. When he left, I remember taking a moment in my office to think about how wrong I had been. Thinking back to my initial impression of Rasheed, it was like I was judging a tree in winter. How unfair is it to judge a tree when its limbs are bare and it is dormant? My students taught me that if you wait a little while, spring will come. Judging someone too early, in the wrong season, robs them of opportunities. And as a coach, it puts you in a place of judge and critic rather than supporter and cheerleader.

Rasheed was one of the first clients who first helped me see that the initial impressions we make of people are not accurate. In fact, they are often far from accurate. Though we all fall victim to the urge to judge people from our first impressions, Examiners, of all the interview styles, are the most likely to do so. This is because they use "expert mind," meaning that they believe they are experts, like I used to, which can make it hard for them to accurately gauge other people. In Nicholas Epley's book, *Mindwise: Why We Misunderstand What Others Think, Believe, Feel, and Want*, he illustrates how bad we are at mind reading. He argues that the more confident you think you will be at reading other people's minds, the less likely you are to make accurate predictions about what other people think. Confidence equals inaccuracy. When I made judgments of Rasheed, I did so from a confidence that I was right because of my experience, but my confidence got in the way of seeing his potential.

When Examiners are in their expert mind, they come across as technically proficient but they then have a tendency, the way I did with Rasheed, to see an interview as pass or fail which doesn't give them room to practice, explore, and enjoy the process. Giving themselves very little room for error or improvisation, the Examiner falls prey to expert mind, believing that there is only one way to do it correctly, and any small mistake, infraction, or slipup will cost them mightily. Believing something is a certain way before you even give it a chance to show you what it is, is like judging a tree in winter.

Why Examiners Need to Get It Right

Examiners hold themselves to high standards and assume that they are being judged harshly, and they fear that they will look like an idiot in front of people whose opinions they care about, people whom they respect or who hold the power to give them a job. They believe that the result of a job interview is binary: you either get the job or you don't. That it's a test that they will either pass or fail. To put it into perspective, Charmers view interviews as more fluid; they see them as an opportunity to start a relationship. Examiners' binary view of interviewing enforces their need to be perfect, which can hold them back and make them uneasy.

Examiners also want to get it right because they want to conserve their resources. As an Examiner put it, "What's the purpose of doing it if it isn't done right?" If Examiners are going to put in the effort to go through the "dog and pony show," then they better get it right; they better get the job, otherwise it wasn't worth it.

In *How to Be Yourself: How to Quiet Your Inner Critic and Rise Above Social Anxiety*, Ellen Hendriksen, PhD, calls that need for perfection our inner critic. She explains that "the critic wants you to do better, to be perfect, so it pushes you to perform while at the same time undermining your faith in your ability. Your flawless social performance is somehow supposed to emerge effortlessly and fully formed." Examiners suffer from the pressure of their inner critic, demanding perfection from themselves, which isn't possible without the process of trying and failing first. Obviously, our inner critic and this need to be perfect becomes limiting. Examiners need to quiet their inner critic so they can allow themselves to try.

How Examiners Can Manage Their Need to Get It Right

In interviewing, you will experience all kinds of situations with all kinds of people whose experience level varies widely. As someone who has been interviewing for over twenty years, I have never seen the exact situation twice; to expect that there is a right and wrong way is to set yourself up for failure, disappointment, and misaligned expectations. I've learned that most people have never been trained to interview, most people wing it, and no one follows a guidebook because there isn't one. The Examiner's fear of getting it wrong reminds me of a friend of mine who will not dance. She is convinced that she will look like a fool. Interviewing, like dancing, is an experience-based process. It is *not* a test, and you can't get it right.

Interviews are exploratory. Interviews teach you a tremendous amount about yourself. If you interview poorly, you will learn how to do it differently. If you interview well, you will learn what works. You may repeat exactly what you did before that went so well, only for that approach to miss the mark with different people. And just because you interview well and they offer you the job doesn't mean you will want it; you may learn in the interview that you don't like the job or company or the hiring manager. You may go through the process only to realize you don't want to leave your current job. There are so many possibilities beyond not getting hired or getting hired. Being open to these other possibilities will make the interview process more enjoyable and actually improves your chances. You can gain more than a job from the interview process.

 INTERVIEW PRINCIPLE FOR JOB SEEKERS

An interview is not just about getting a job. It can also be an exercise in learning what you want for your career. Just as you notice things you like during an interview, pay attention to things that you don't like—aspects of the role, qualities of the hiring manager, or details related to the company culture. These will help inform your decisions and help you eventually end up in the job that is right for you.

As an Examiner told me, "I am very stubborn, and I think my way is the best way, but a few years out of school I realized my approach was illogical. If I am not willing to change, I will be wrong more often than I will be right. It was that realization that made me open up to other possibilities that I wasn't open to before. I guess you could say I became more open-minded based on principle and logic, because I couldn't stand to be wrong, but that's how I got there."

In interviews, like dancing, we must risk looking like a fool. Improving is part of the process. The only way to get better and have a chance at getting the job is by putting yourself out there, and you can't do it by sitting on the side of the dance floor. You can enjoy things without them being perfect. And there is no way of getting good at interviews by not putting yourself out there. Author and life coach Martha Beck said it best: "Getting over your fear without doing anything scary is like learning to swim before you go near the water—it'd be nice if such a thing were possible, but it ain't."

Examiners are uncomfortable being vulnerable; that's why they arm themselves with the facts. Separate yourself from the idea of perfection, from the black-and-white approach, and adopt a more primal, natural way, one that embraces our common humanity and vulnerability. Try not to take yourself too seriously. Remember that no one is as hard on you as you are. You can use this opportunity to beat yourself up and hold yourself to high standards, or you can use this as an opportunity to learn if your approach works, to change up your style, to try something new, to prepare differently. This process can be exciting.

An Examiner's obsession with perfection is isolating. The right way has only one answer. A more inclusive approach is more connected to the whole. Examiners have an opposite style that they should look at to help them enjoy the process. When it comes to relaxing their ideas of perfection, they should look to Charmers. As I mentioned, Charmers do not look at interviews as pass or fail; they see them as opportunities to get to know someone, the first step in a relationship. When you look at it this way, you take the pressure off yourself.

Examiners will feel better when they recognize that there isn't one way to do it. That there are a lot of people who have different approaches and not only survive but also get the jobs.

There is no such thing as perfection. But the only way to make yourself proud is to move forward despite uncertainty, despite mistakes and setbacks. Confidence comes from doing it. Not perfectly, not exactly, just doing it. There is a freedom in that: you don't have to be perfect to gain momentum to learn a lesson or move forward; all you have to do is do it. One small step at a time. The idea of perfection is an illusion, so don't let it hold you back. Take action no matter how frightened you are.

You can only do the best you can. If you do the best you can, prepare, and do the work, you will make yourself proud, and that is better than chasing an elusive, unattainable goal of perfection.

When Examiners Interview Well

When Examiners interview well, they balance their need to get it right with a practiced professionalism. They are great listeners because they don't always need to be the star of the show. They show they are qualified by being exact, through answers that are not long-winded but rather precise and factual. Charmers excel in storytelling, Challengers excel in investigating, and an Examiner, when they interview well, excels at being the expert. They are specific, unambiguous, and particular, which generates a feeling of stability.

When an Examiner interviews well they balance their need to be seen as the expert with a capacity to reveal their insecurities. They understand that to be good at interviewing, not only do you have to be seen as technically capable, but you have to get to know the other people, and the best way to do that is to show your humanity. They understand that there is no such thing as perfection. And the best Examiner lets down their guard and allows others in, even if just for moment, to connect.

When Examiners Interview Poorly

When an Examiner interviews poorly, it's because they are not opening up. They avoid small talk. They give very short answers to questions they deem unproductive and insincere. They focus only on what they think is important and provide very short answers that give the impression that they are not interested. To a recruiter or hiring manager asking interview questions, it feels as though you are pulling teeth to get them to talk to you.

Examiners' fear of getting it wrong prevents them from opening up. Examiners are not comfortable talking about themselves and they do not go into an interview wanting to be liked; they rely too heavily on how they do the job, not *why*. In essence, they don't go out of their comfort zone. They play it so safe; they give so little room for detail or interpretation that they are seen as one-dimensional. By playing it so close to the vest, they eliminate all of their personality from their answers. Soft skills take a back seat. They sanitize themselves. They make it all technical, but stories are where we connect. Stories make your points come to life. You can get your point across without just reporting it but rather telling it as a story. Think back to your favorite teachers: Did they just stand at the front of the classroom and tell you the lesson, or did they make it interesting? The best way for someone to remember you and remember how you are qualified is by telling them a story—in this case, *your* story.

When Examiners interview poorly, they may look at an interview like a transaction and withhold smiles or pleasantries. Yes, someone who is interviewing you is doing their job, and they will get paid to do it, but an Examiner needs to accept that we all have needs that go beyond money. There is a strong need for people to feel useful, noticed, and appreciated, even when they are doing their job. Examiners are impatient with small gestures. They think, *How far does a compliment really go? Why should I make someone feel good when the purpose of the interview is to show that I am good at the job, not good at being nice?*

Essentially, Examiners only want the interview to be about work, and anything that deviates feels like a great imposition, a great compromise, and when an Examiner interviews poorly it's because they refuse to make that compromise.

Examiners have lofty goals and could benefit from small acts of warmth. They need to remember that you can change someone's perspective of you by a small act of vulnerability to show your humanity. Not everything has to be on a large scale.

How to Interview an Examiner Job Seeker

Examiners think that getting the hiring manager to see them as capable is the most important factor to being hired, so they prioritize talking about the job, their transferable skills, and how they could improve the process.

Examiners report rather than connect. Examiners do not need small talk and in fact prefer to just have technical interviews that are geared toward your specialized knowledge. To an Examiner, a conversational interview feels like a waste of time and not nearly as important as the technical interviews. To an Examiner, the most important aspect of an interview is figuring out what the job is and if they can do it. When faced with small talk, they will engage begrudgingly, and they will not tell you a lot. A client once told me that an HR recruiter asked about his thoughts on where he lived and he said he grew bored and irritated because none of those questions had anything to do with whether or not he could do the job. I countered that perhaps she was a Charmer and she was looking to connect; my client agreed but went on to say, "I gave her the answer, but I was annoyed because what does that have to do with the job?"

It's important to know that it's not that they don't like you or that they aren't interested in the job, they just do not think it is relevant. In order to get an Examiner to open up, start with the interview questions and end with the small talk. Make sure you make the small-talk questions somewhat relevant to the job because Examiners are unwilling to share anything that is not on their resume.

If you ask an Examiner job seeker, "Tell me about a time you did x," they will always choose to talk about their processes, methods, and tools. Examiners don't talk about the team they were on, not because their team wasn't important, but because they just think it's implied. Rather, their answers will reflect their qualifications because their top priority is to see if they can do the job. They want to confirm that the job description matches up to what the hiring manager says they need.

Examiners want to know about the job itself, the roles and responsibilities, how their skills transfer, how they will fit in, or how they could improve the process. They will ask questions about the job description and your needs so they can tell you how they are qualified. Unlike Charmers, who will tell you why they want the job, an Examiner will tell you how they will do it. Ask them to elaborate on why they want the job, not just how they can do the job. Be specific if you want to know something. Ask better questions that are derived from the competencies required in the job description. Get to know the nuances of what a candidate has done previously to get a good understanding of how they will perform.

How to Interview with an Examiner Hiring Manager

Examiners have a tendency to conduct an interview like they are testing someone. They can come across as cold and intimidating. An Examiner hiring manager may take on a haughty tone and internalized distance and learned caution. Perhaps they require people whom they interview with to stay on a script, with a very structured approach. They may not like someone who makes a confession of vulnerability or approaches them with interest and dares to ask them anything deeply personal.

An Examiner hiring manager focuses on the experience a candidate has, what projects they have done, and their day-to-day responsibilities. Ultimately, they care about what skills are transferable. From there, they determine if you have what it takes to do the job. It is not necessarily a deal breaker for an Examiner if you don't have the exact experience they are looking for, but they will need clear data on how your experience makes you a good fit.

Examiners are listening to your answers carefully and don't like off-the-cuff responses; they want you to be prepared. They're going to ask the same questions to every candidate no matter what. Examiners aren't going to get conversational, and they aren't going to change up their interview questions midstream.

You won't fully persuade an Examiner with eagerness and passion; you have to back it up. Prove some level of competence by talking about your qualifications, use metrics, and support your desire for the job with some tangible evidence as to why you'd be a good fit. If you build on what they say and just tell a story, you will leave the Examiner wanting more.

Above all else, Examiners want to be certain. So make your answers clear, precise, and to the point.

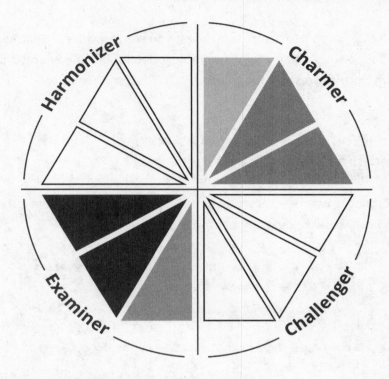

How an Examiner Interviews with Their Opposite—the Charmer

Charmers prioritize making a connection, and they are very expressive with both their verbal and nonverbal communication. Charmers adjust their behavior and their style depending on who they are with, unlike Examiners, who are steadfast in their approach. Charmers are often eager and full of enthusiasm, and this may be off-putting because Examiners may think it is insincere. Charmers want Examiners to open up; they require you to talk not just about your work experience but also your opinions and thoughts. By nature, Examiners question things, and they may tend to take a more skeptical approach when interviewing, which is the polar opposite of Charmer's optimistic and open approach. Examiners will need to push themselves out of their comfort zone. Examiners may rely on sitting back and observing, but to a Charmer that means you aren't involved. Charmers will require Examiners to share not just details, but the energy that they normally reserve for people much closer to them.

How You Can Balance Your Approach and Tap into the Other Styles

Examiners can be more successful if they pull traits from other styles to balance out their natural tendencies:

- *Examiners can learn to be accommodating and enjoy the process of getting to know someone the way a Charmer does.*
- *Examiners can allow themselves to open up the way a Challenger does.*
- *Examiners can tap into the adaptability and easygoing-ness of Harmonizers to get their point across.*

Advice for Examiners	**Pre-interview Mantras for Examiners to Manage Their Need to Get It Right.**
It pays to connect.	"It may not be perfect, but I will try my best." "Even if I don't get the job, I will learn something." "I will showcase all of myself."

Key Takeaways for Examiner Job Seekers

- Relying on your qualifications may land you the job, but you aren't there to just recite your resume. You need to bring your resume to life. Who you are and why you do what you do matters a lot. It's not a liability to share these things in an interview. Don't be afraid to share stories and more about yourself that isn't on your resume.

- Don't limit yourself to the mindset that you will either get the job or not. Look at it this way: you may not get the job, but you will get practice at interviewing and learn more about what you want, the types of companies and how they hire, and ultimately you will get better at interviewing the more you do it. It's not a loss if you don't get the job. Experience is valuable either way.

Key Takeaways for Examiner Hiring Managers

- This is not a test; it is the beginning of a relationship with a person.

- You will be attracted to candidates who are primarily focused on results and their qualifications, but you may overlook their personality. Remember, this person has to fit into the culture, serve your clients, and work with coworkers. They are not just a tool to get a job done, they are a whole person, and you need to discover who that person is in the interview to determine if they will succeed in the role.

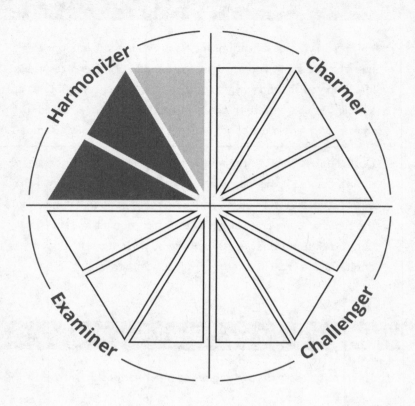

Harmonizer. Their goal is to put others at ease. They are focused externally and seek approval from others. They are often quiet and humble and slow to warm, but once they open up are quite engaging. They are thoughtful and like to contribute to what the interviewer is saying. They rarely if ever push the boundaries. It's important to them that they come across as easygoing and low-maintenance. They see asking for stuff as a great imposition. They want to be liked and to get along with everyone they meet.

11

Harmonizer

"I want to adapt."

On a cold, overcast November afternoon in 2016, I was in a classroom teaching an interview skills workshop at Temple's Fox School of Business, when I felt my right arm get tingly. I thought maybe my arm went to sleep because of the way I was sitting. A few minutes later, I was midsentence, looking at the classroom of seniors who were all eagerly hanging on to my every word about how to negotiate, when all of a sudden my leg went numb. I paused and thought, *Why is the entire right side of my body numb?* Never one to cut a class short, I finished the workshop and drove myself directly to the emergency room.

In a full suit, I lay on a stretcher, thinking that I must be having a stroke. As my mind wandered to the most catastrophic and horrible outcomes, I forced myself not to search WebMD and waited for the doctor. The nurses performed all the tests. Everything seemed normal, but I didn't feel normal. My right side was still numb—my face, my arm, and my leg. At this point, they had been numb for hours. I recalled the moment finding my grandfather after his stroke, and a flood of awful memories came back to me. As I fought back tears, the emergency room chief of medicine walked in. He was a quiet, unassuming man with a tender bedside manner. He sat on the side of my stretcher and started in with the small talk. He asked me what I'd been doing when the numbness started, and I told him I was teaching. He asked what I taught, and for a moment I was embarrassed to say *interviewing*. I looked at my feet, my burgundy high heels sticking out of the hospital blanket, and struggled to answer because I felt like my work was insignificant compared to a doctor's, but I said, "I teach hiring managers and students how to interview better." I will never forget the doctor's reaction: he pulled his head away and said, "Oh, wow, I need to know how to do what you do. I am so bad at interviews. They terrify me!" What? How can that be? This, coming from a man who went to medical school and runs an emergency room, which I imagine to be one the toughest work environments, shocked me. I thought, *How can you triage emergency medical care and see the worst of humanity every day but interviews scare you?* He went on to say, "I just never know what they want me to say, and I get so nervous."

He was a Harmonizer. Quiet and unassuming, with a great bedside manner, but he and I joked that what made him good with patients didn't make him good at interviewing. He shared that he hates selling himself and would rather talk to someone about who they are than tell someone what he can do. He said he'd only had a few interviews and avoids them like the plague, but that avoiding them had held him back and made him even more afraid to try.

As I left the emergency room undiagnosed, saddled with my own fear that I was exhibiting the first symptoms of MS or Parkinson's, I reflected on my conversation with the doctor and wondered how he could be so terrified of interviews when he faces much worse every day. We all fear what we don't have experience with. The unknown is scary. Interviews are comfortable for me because I have been in so many (over ten thousand), in the same way standing at the bedside of a sick patient is comfortable for him because he's done it tens of thousands of times.

After my MRI came back negative for all the worst possible diagnoses and I was diagnosed with hemiplegic migraines, body migraines that cause temporary weakness on one side of the body, I felt like I had a new lease on life, and with that, a new appreciation for what I do.

Harmonizers See Interviews as a Tryout

The doctor who treated me was a Harmonizer, which gave him a kind and reassuring bedside manner. However, the very skill that made him so good at his job is one that can get in the way of him getting jobs, and it's the same for other Harmonizers because, more than any other style, Harmonizers prioritize their audience, which presents unique challenges in interviews. Harmonizers want to fit in, they want to adapt, and they want to get along. They do this by holding back, by making assumptions about what the interviewer wants and adjusting their attitudes to fit those assumptions. Like Charmers, they seek the approval of the interviewer and want to be liked. They want to fit in, but unlike Charmers, they are introverts. They do not make a show in the same way a Charmer does. They sell themselves by being easygoing and interested in how they can add to the team. They are the polar opposite of the Challenger. Unlike a Challenger, who asks tough questions and doesn't mind playing the devil's advocate, a Harmonizer will not rock the boat. A Harmonizer's goal is to put others at ease. They are less worried about themselves; they care about the comfort and needs of others.

A hiring manager, Amanda, confessed to me during a prep session before an interview, "I have a hard time talking with strangers, or worse, emailing people that I don't know, because I don't know if I should be friendly or straight to the point. I don't know what they want, and I want to be what they want." I suggested that she might be overthinking it a bit and asked if she could be herself. She laughed and said, "I am a total overthinker when it comes to what other people want and need. I can get paralyzed with fear and uncertainty. It holds me back."

What Amanda does is what a lot of Harmonizers do, diminish their own needs to make a better impression. Harmonizers want everyone to get along, and they are so good at being accommodating, but that can backfire on them. Harmonizers can be so concerned with their audience that they lose themselves. Harmonizers overprioritize their audience and, when they don't have one, become paralyzed, don't perform well, and sometimes even bail. Many Harmonizers have reported that they feel lost without an audience, that they don't know how to act if they don't know the structure of an interaction and lose their voice when no one is around. This is because Harmonizers base who they are on those around them.

Harmonizers can investigate their discomfort to help them get to the core of what they want, versus what they think others want from them. With Amanda, I started by asking her, "How would you act if you didn't have an audience?" The question scared her. "How would you be if you were just being yourself?" She was unsure, so I suggested, "Let's create a strategy that feels authentic to you so when you have to email someone you won't feel as paralyzed. For instance, when you get a really friendly email, how does it make you feel?"

"Good," she said.

"Okay, so would you like to make that same impression and make someone else feel good?" She nodded. "So when you send an email introducing yourself, be friendly."

"Well, it's not that simple; what if the other person isn't that type? What if they don't like to get friendly emails?"

"I love how empathetic and considerate you are, but is it possible that you are putting other people first? Could you be basing who you are too much on what you think others need?" She agreed and shared that it was hard for her to trust that if she was herself she could attract the right candidates. She had always molded herself to fit what she assumed others wanted, and hiring was no exception.

Interviews are a place where you need to sell yourself. You can't sell yourself if you don't tell someone WHO you are—you are the most important part of your story. Of all the interview styles, Harmonizers have the hardest time with this. First, because they would rather give people what they want than put themselves out there or be seen as demanding. Second, they have a hard time owning their successes. Harmonizers are more comfortable talking about you, your team, and your goals, but not their own.

 INTERVIEW PRINCIPLE FOR JOB SEEKERS

You can't sell yourself if you don't tell someone *who* you are—you are the most important part of your story.

Harmonizers are uncomfortable drawing a line in the sand, putting themselves out there and telling someone who they are, what they want, and why. But knowing who you are and what you want is critical to succeeding and getting what you want. This is especially true in an interview. A hiring manager will ask you tough questions; they will want to know what you've done and why. They want to get to know the real you to see if you'll be a good fit for the team. Harmonizers can learn from their opposite, the Challenger, who easily tells someone who they are and prioritizes feeling heard and respected.

Anita

I've known Anita for over fifteen years. We worked in our first HR jobs together. I know her as a colleague, client, and friend. She is warm and accepting. She practices yoga, and she embodies the spirit of Buddha. She is calm and unwavering in her commitment to help others. She went to school for social work and, after a draining stint working with juveniles in the criminal justice system, she went into HR. That's when I met her, over fifteen years ago, when she was very pregnant with her first child. We worked in a tiny HR office, elbow to elbow. I left that role to work in the city as a recruiter, and she stayed for a little while longer, then left for another HR job with a bigger office.

As her baby grew into a little boy, so did her career from HR generalist to HR business partner. She got a job in the pharmaceutical industry. She was great at her job, which was part social work, part HR. She advocated for employees and provided counseling and a much-needed ear. But the pharmaceutical industry is tough, and they have a lot of layoffs. It became her full-time job to "exit employees." She was great at it, but it was killing her. She needed to get out and find a more stable industry, not just for her growing boy but for her sanity. She needed a culture that reflected her values and needed to be in a job where she could support people and not have to lay them off all the time. She found a seemingly perfect company. A very reliable organization that never laid people off.

Anita is a Harmonizer. In the interview for the new job, she held back because she wanted to see how the company presented themselves, how they interviewed, and what the culture was like. She was comfortable letting them take the lead. She didn't prepare for the interview; she went into it to "feel them out." She believed, as most Harmonizers do, that she simply couldn't prepare for an interview because the best answer would come to her when she was able to read the room and the interviewer's body language. She confessed to me that her approach almost always works, except when the interviewer has a poker face. Then she said, "I don't have anything to go on. Because I go off what they say and how they act." Harmonizers prioritize adapting and fitting in. They see interviews as a tryout for a team.

The interview went well, and they made her an offer. She called me to go over it and help her decide if she should take the job. Her main requirement at the time was to not have to lay people off, and she wanted more security herself. The company checked those two boxes. I asked her if that was all she needed; she said yes.

She had gone into the interview with little research and no preconceived notions. Her entire agenda was to get a feel for the company. She only had one interview and, by her admission, they were more focused on getting their questions answered than sharing much about the company. She admitted that a feeling might not be enough to base a big decision on, but she was sick of her current job, so she accepted the position.

Six years later, with her son now entering high school, she's found herself unhappy again. The qualities that make her an asset to the team are also the qualities that make her feel isolated, ostracized, and alone. The company she works for doesn't share her harmonizing qualities—they are not easygoing or concerned with the team. The vast majority of the organization are her opposites. Whereas Anita is more flexible and accommodating, they pride themselves on putting a stake in the ground and asking tough questions. There is no doubt that they need her, but they don't make it easy for her.

As a Harmonizer, it is difficult for her to ask for what she wants. In the interview she didn't stand up for herself and say what she needed to be successful. She learned a very valuable lesson: it's important to be easygoing, but it's equally important to know who you are and what you want, and to advocate for that.

Approach and Style

Harmonizers believe that other people's opinions hold more value than their own; they prioritize other people because they want to fit in. They want to be liked for being easygoing. The first five minutes of an interview is very important for them, as they assess the situation and the people they are interviewing with to see what approach to take. They do not go into an interview wanting or planning to take the lead. They want to see how it goes, how it develops, and what happens. Their approach can be described as *passive observation*.

Harmonizers take their cues from the interviewer. They mirror and mimic their attitudes and interests to make a good impression. They believe that imitation is the sincerest form of flattery, that the best way to show that they will be a good fit for the team is to act like the team. They adapt easily, unlike Challengers and Examiners, who don't adapt to what the interviewer is saying.

Harmonizers often struggle with owning their story, in part because their approach to an interview is that a new job is a clean slate, a fresh start, and a new beginning. They believe that talking about their past jobs is irrelevant. They don't want to be known for what they did in the past; they want to talk about potential and what they can do in the future. Harmonizers would rather be asked very specific questions about the job they are interviewing for rather than general questions about the past. For example, a common way to begin interviews is by asking a candidate, "Can you walk me through your work experience?" Harmonizers cringe at this question; instead they would rather be asked, "If we were to hire you, could you walk us through what you would do to learn the new role in the first thirty, sixty, and ninety days?" Harmonizers are very tuned in to relevance. *Is this important to the job I am interviewing for? What does this have to do with the job you are hiring for?*

While they prefer specific interview questions, Harmonizers aren't known for being transparent, making their wishes known—they can be hard to figure out. They are quiet chameleons. Their need to fit in and desire to talk about the future makes it hard for people to pin them down, and they like it that way.

Harmonizers do not want to take the time in an interview to talk about themselves. They want to listen, observe, and add to what someone else has said. Harmonizers are selfless in a way that Charmers are selfish. While Harmonizers want to become part of something because they love the idea of being on a team, Charmers want to become part of something so they can show what they can do.

This need to be part of the team and fit into a culture isn't one that should be dismissed as them not having a strong sense of who they are. Their wish to talk about the future rather than the past doesn't mean that they don't have a grasp on what they've done; they just don't think it's relevant to what they want to do next. They just have a different priority: becoming part of something bigger than themselves. This need, this drive, often leads them to make a great impression. They want to fit into the culture, they have a desire to be great team players, and they want to make the world an easier place to live in. Those qualities are traditionally positively reinforced in workers. We want to hire people who buy into the mission and want to work toward the greater goal.

Harmonizers like Anita believe that they will make the best impression by deferring to the interviewer. They show their interest not by reciting their qualifications like an Examiner or asking tough questions like a Challenger or being eager like a Charmer. Harmonizers sell themselves by being agreeable, flexible, and thoughtful. They show their value by listening. They create an impression of care. They are very sensitive to the needs of others, and they avoid making someone feel awkward or embarrassed at all costs, even if that cost is them not getting the job. They'd rather take the risk to be seen as making a mistake than correct something and potentially embarrass someone.

It's hard for them to ask tough questions and test someone. So they can have trouble as hiring mangers because they do not want to put someone on the spot.

I once taught executives at a retreat how to interview, and when one Harmonizer read his Interviewology Profile interview style, he said, "I sound like a lap dog." I asked him to elaborate. "I do take into consideration other people, and I do care more about the team, but I don't think that is what I am supposed to care about as an executive. Aren't I supposed to be more demanding, more hard, more full of myself?"

I said, "You bring fantastic qualities to your job. It's your bias that limits how you think about it. Perhaps you have bought into some idea of how an executive is 'supposed' to act, but you are an executive and you don't act that way." He agreed that perhaps he wasn't giving himself enough credit. Harmonizers have a tendency to do that.

Harmonizers are equanimous, which I think makes a great leader. They are calm under pressure. They are thoughtful, and they are magnanimous. They are not overly enthusiastic the way a Charmer tends to be. They are measured. But this can sometimes make them look disinterested and unprepared.

Their interest in the team above themselves can prevent them from owning their story. I met a client once who told me that he wanted to prepare for the interview but didn't want to make it about him. I laughed and then realized that he was serious. Whatever the situation, he thought he could make a better impression if he kept the conversation about someone else. You can't do that in an interview. Whether you are a job seeker or hiring manager, you need to know who you are and what you want. And people need to get to know *you*. Harmonizers downplay their strengths and overemphasize other people. In the way an Examiner needs to bring their whole self to an interview highlighting their personality as well as their qualifications, a Harmonizer needs to adopt a more *I/me* vocabulary rather than a *we/us* one.

Charmers take making an impression very seriously. They are showmen and want the performance to be flawless, from the clothes they wear to their body language—everything is carefully considered, whereas Harmonizers do not think about making an impression in that way. Some Harmonizers that I have worked with have gotten feedback that they didn't take their interview attire seriously. And it's not because they don't care about how someone sees them, it's because they don't want the spotlight on them. They want to make the impression that they are more interested in learning about the other person, the job, and the company. Their intention is to blend in and to adapt, and sometimes they try to do that with their clothes. It's not disinterest in their presentation, it's just not wanting it to be about them. Not wanting to stand out.

Some Harmonizers can make this work if they are in an industry that doesn't prioritize the way someone dresses in an interview. But imagine a Harmonizer, who downplays their own strengths and doesn't dress to impress, in an interview for a hedge fund on Wall Street. Imagine a Harmonizer who interviews to find out about other people and doesn't consider that their clothes will matter at an interview for a design firm. In some jobs and some industries, the clothes you wear matter, and a little bit of ego is expected—it's a qualification that the interviewer looks for.

Harmonizers are very good at mimicking the interviewer. If they interview with an expressive person who really takes the lead, this approach can go well because they have a lot to go off of. But when they interview with someone who may be serious or not wear their emotions on their sleeve, they are left without any cues and may feel lost.

One Harmonizer told me, "I interviewed with this woman once: she didn't let on about anything. She asked questions like a robot and never gave me any nonverbal feedback. She didn't smile, she didn't wince, nothing. It was so off-putting. I didn't have anything to use, I didn't know how to be, because I always played off the other person." Ultimately, basing how you portray yourself off of your interviewer is not the best approach because in the process, you get lost.

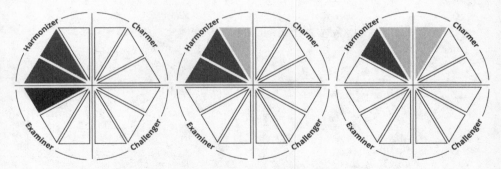

From left to right: Harmonizer with Examiner tendencies, Harmonizer, and Harmonizer with Charmer tendencies

Harmonizer Variations

Like all interview styles, there is variation within the Harmonizer style. As you can see in the interview style hexagon, Harmonizers are closest to Examiners and Charmers, and often share traits with these styles.

TRAITS HARMONIZERS SHARE WITH EXAMINERS

- *Reserved*
- *Not going to volunteer something that is not on their resume*
- *Introverted; provide access to just their public persona and work life*
- *Slow to warm*
- *Think to speak*
- *Quiet*
- *Answers are short and to the point*
- *Don't lead conversations*
- *Solve problems by thinking them through*

TRAITS HARMONIZERS SHARE WITH CHARMERS

- People focused
- Externally focused
- Accommodating and flexible
- Charm
- Know how their personality fits into the company culture
- Believe anyone can be persuaded, live by the motto charm works
- Make a good impression by being friendly, likeable, and relatable
- Comfortable with ambiguity, can improvise
- Comfortable selling themselves
- Confidence comes from social desirability
- Like small talk and conversation
- Change style and answers to fit others
- Rely on soft skills
- Don't like when the interview is only technical
- Need chitchat to break tension and decrease their nerves; need rapport to put them at ease

Because of this overlap, in addition to the Harmonizer style, there are also two variations of Harmonizers: Harmonizer/Examiner and Harmonizer/Charmer. Let's look a bit closer at what differentiates the three types of Harmonizers.

Harmonizer with Examiner Tendencies

Harmonizer with Examiner tendencies is an introvert who's accommodating with steadfast tendencies. They are more precise than any of the other Harmonizer styles. They hold back until something piques their interest and will get involved in a conversation only if the topic interests them. They are more likely to observe the conversation if others are talking. They do not steer the conversation to them or change the subject. Their conversational style is about others; they do not talk about themselves or share details that are personal. They are private, quiet, and unassuming. Harmonizers with Examiner tendencies never take the lead. They prioritize fitting in, what others need from them, and how they would fit into the culture, unlike Charmers, for instance, who focus on how the company can benefit from them.

Harmonizer

A Harmonizer (without any variation) is introverted and accommodating. An interview is not a natural setting for an introvert because they are not generally ready to open up to someone within a few minutes of meeting them. They are private and keep their emotions and enthusiasm to themselves. They play it close to the vest. Of all the interview styles, Harmonizers are the most willing to adapt. They prefer unstructured interviews that feel conversational. They think to speak, so they require time to prepare their thoughts and answers. Since they are more quiet than the other styles, they often ask more insightful questions and are generally more thoughtful and better listeners. Harmonizers are externally focused, and their style changes based on who they are interviewing with. They prioritize adapting, getting along, and not "rocking the boat." They make a good impression by being easygoing.

Harmonizer with Charmer Tendencies

A Harmonizer with Charmer tendencies is an introvert with accommodating tendencies. They are the most open Harmonizer. When they are not in a setting that calls for them to be outgoing, they prefer to be quiet. They have a tendency to balance out the interviewer, so if they are being interviewed by an extrovert, they may become more introverted, and vice versa. Charmers with Harmonizer tendencies let the more dominant personality take the lead. They hold back until something piques their interest, more likely to get involved in a conversation if the topic appeals to them. They are more likely to observe the conversation if others are talking. They do not steer the conversation to them or change the subject if it doesn't interest them; context has to be right for them to seek attention. Charmer/Harmonizers charm by being thoughtful.

How to Tell If You Are Talking to a Harmonizer

- Harmonizers listen.

- They are accepting.

- Harmonizers enjoy getting to know you.

- They come across as warm and collaborative.

- They withhold, especially with people they don't know or in situations where the power dynamic is skewed.

- Harmonizers are afraid of rocking the boat and not fitting in.

- Interviewing is a tryout for a team they want to join.

- Harmonizers get you to see them as qualified by being agreeable.

(For practice identifying the different styles, see the Deciphering the Interview Styles activity in the Appendix.)

Strengths and Overused Strengths

Harmonizers have many strengths, but when they are out of balance, their intentions can be misinterpreted. The following table looks at their strengths and how those strengths can appear when they are overused.

Strengths	Overused Strengths
Resourceful	Unprepared
Flexible	Too flexible, no backbone
Agreeable	Lacking their own opinions
Observant	Doesn't contribute
Sensitive	Withholding
Happy to go along for the ride	Follower, lacking their own direction
External focus	Prioritizes others over themselves

12

Interviewing with a Harmonizer

I didn't want to start this book by telling my story. I don't want people to know me as the girl who moved out at fifteen. I have strived to be successful so I could leave that all behind me. For a long time, I never told anyone. It wasn't something I wanted people to know about me. I wanted them to know me for who I'd made myself into, not who I had been. I was afraid that people would pity me and feel sorry for me and do things for me because they thought I needed help.

I was afraid that people would judge me.

When I told the admissions officer at Penn my story, it was one of the last times I ever told anyone. Until I was asked to speak at DisruptHR.

DisruptHR is a five-minute talk for HR professionals where speakers are encouraged to push the envelope, swear, and be provocative. Not really my professional style, so I took a more tell-all approach and wrote a speech about how the hiring process is flawed. Then I had a networking call with a woman who works at an economic development nonprofit whose goal is to help college students get jobs in and stay in Philadelphia. Our missions are closely aligned, and we have a lot in common personally and professionally. We had a wonderful conversation that went on for over an hour. We discovered that we have kids the same age and so many shared life experiences. At the end of the call, she asked me to be on a panel to discuss the challenges that first-generation college students face. I said, "I'd love to, but that is the same day that I am scheduled to do DisruptHR. I really wish I could, because although I am not first-generation I really resonate with those issues because I moved out at fifteen, and I know what it's like to have to work and pay rent while you're in college."

She said, "I really hope that's what your DisruptHR talk is about."

I laughed, "No. Absolutely not. I don't tell anyone that story. I can't believe I just told you." She said, "You should. It's so inspiring and amazing." I was dumbfounded and concluded that she was being nice. I told my partner about the call, and he encouraged me to do it, but it still didn't feel like a good idea.

Then I slept on it, and I woke up wondering if they might be on to something. The few times I'd talked about it, opening up like that made me proud. Perhaps I had gained enough professional credibility that I could do it. Perhaps I was brave enough now to be vulnerable. I sat down at my computer and wrote a new speech. Once it was written, I worried about what people would think, but part of me really liked the speech.

I practiced with friends and almost cried. They encouraged me with every round of practice. I recited it on my walk to work, in the shower, and before bed. Anytime I had a spare five minutes, I worked on memorizing it. With each round of practice, I got comfortable. When the day came, I had no reservations about the content.

The night of, I was the ninth presenter out of eleven. I was excited about the opportunity, but there was a nagging part of me that wondered if I was making the right professional decision. What would my clients think? What would my employees think? They were all there in the audience. There were over 250 people in the room, and I knew more than fifty of them personally. What was I thinking?

I walked out on the stage and told my story. In front of all those people, under those lights, I let myself be seen. My whole self. All of it. I owned my story publicly for the first time.

Afterward, people came up to me to congratulate me on a job well done. To shake my hand. To introduce themselves to me. There was this one woman who waited patiently at the back of the crowd. When the crowd dissipated, she approached me and grabbed me by both shoulders and said, "Thank you for telling your story." I wasn't prepared for that. Honestly, I was barely prepared to tell it, let alone have someone thank me for telling it. I was so bowled over I said, "You're thanking me? I should be thanking you. Thanks for coming." She noticed that I was brushing past her compliment, and this time she shook my shoulders, which she continued to hold, and said, "By you doing that up there on that stage, by you telling your story, it made me feel like I can tell mine. Thank you!" I was speechless. I'd never thought of it that way. I'd always just thought about my own potential embarrassment and shame. I'd never considered that if I shared my difficulties it would make it easier for others to do the same. I always saw it as *my* story, but when you tell your story, you connect with others and become part of their story.

It took me twenty-five years to get there. It took me almost a decade teaching people to interview to fully grasp the real reason I do it. Yes, I love interviewing, but what I really do is empower people to tell their story.

And I know the power of owning your story. For years, I wished that it hadn't happened to me. Then I wished that success would make up for it. Then I figured if I moved on and had my own family and was a great parent to my kids, then I would magically make it disappear. But none of that worked. What worked was looking back and realizing that who I am is the person that made those good choices, that earned that success and was inspired and driven to be a great parent, and that came from the experience that for so long I wanted to pretend never happened. I realized that owning my whole story is where the true power lies.

This is what I hope to teach everyone, but Harmonizers especially. We are not just a fraction of our story. We are not just the part that we want to portray to the world. Not in an interview, and not with our friends, or our spouses, or even our bosses. Whoever you are today is because of what you have overcome, achieved, and earned in the past. To deny your past is to deny the riches that it has given you. And isn't that what life is about? It's about growing and evolving into our highest self, and we can't do that if we think our past is irrelevant.

My story is *my* story. What's yours?

Why Harmonizers Need to Fit In

Wanting to be a part of something bigger than yourself is noble. It's a great quality. Wanting to fit into a culture or team is admirable. Harmonizers are great team players, steady coworkers, and fantastic partners. They focus on the greater good, the bigger picture, and how what they do affects everyone else. They are selfless. They are thoughtful. In an interview this can get in your way. It can prevent you from owning your successes and sharing your individual contributions.

If you are always looking at yourself as a cog in a wheel, a part of a bigger mechanism, it's easy to forget or never take the time to discover what makes *you* unique. In an interview we need to highlight what makes us special, unique, and valuable. We have to answer, "Why should I hire *you*?" or if you are a hiring manager, "Why do I want to work for *you*?" This question, like so many interview questions, is almost impossible to answer if you have never thought deeply about it and answered it for yourself.

And that's just it: Since Harmonizers are so selfless, they don't realize that an interview is all about who they are. Instead, Harmonizers look at it like a tryout for a team they want to join, so they have a tendency to focus their answers on how they will be good for the company.

Harmonizers show their value by thinking of others, not talking about themselves. They may often not take the critical time ahead of an interview to discover what makes them qualified outside being a great team player. I have heard Harmonizers answer almost every interview question with some version of "Whatever you need, I will do it" or "Happy to help wherever I can." They sell their interest in helping but not *how* they can help or, most importantly, how they prefer to work. Since they prioritize adapting, they rarely put a stake in the ground and say, "I prefer customer service." Instead, they would make it about you, the department, or the needs of the company. For an organization that looks for loyal employees that care about the whole over themselves, this style plays really well. However, most interviewers want to see what you can do, not how you fit in. They may interpret your style as insecure or lacking substance.

You may come across, and feel, less confident. In the wonderful book *The Defining Decade*, Meg Jay explains confidence this way: "Confidence doesn't come from the inside out. It moves from the outside in. People feel less anxious—and more confident—on the inside when they can point to things they have done well on the outside." Pointing to your skills isn't only a way to portray confidence; it's also a way to build it. Owning your accomplishments forces you to acknowledge them first—and that can help prove your value to yourself first and foremost.

Like a tryout for a team, Harmonizers tend to focus more on their need to fit in than they focus on making sure that the fit is right for them. They seek the approval of everyone on the team, and they want to be accepted by the company. They show their value by listening and perform better when they have an interviewer to read or go off of. With this strategy, they assume that they will know or glean a lot in an interview from sitting back and taking it all in. But as we already know, there is a significant amount of research that says that we are bad at evaluating other people's thoughts, feelings, and, especially, motives. Because Harmonizers are so singularly focused on being picked for the team, they are at the highest risk of being picked for the wrong team, of adapting so well during the interview that they end up in a position or with a company that was never right for them.

Ultimately, what we all want is to find a job or hire a candidate that will be a good fit long term. We want a place where we can learn and grow and be appreciated for who we are. You will never be appreciated for who you are if you pretend to be something you're not. Until you do the work, until you figure out who *you* are, the fit that you crave will be elusive.

Harmonizers value others over themselves, and that normally leads to self-erasure. They sacrifice a lot of who they are for others, but there is no reward for suffering. Obligations to others, staying with jobs that are beneath us, being underemployed, and staying in relationships with people who deceive us and take advantage do not help us.

Meekness and self-surrender are not kindness. Get comfortable being selfish. To get anything substantial done requires a level of selfishness and priorities. Harmonizers need to find the courage to prioritize themselves and be more forthright with their own dreams, desires, and interests. This is not to make others suffer but so they can save themselves and their resources to serve the world in the best way that they can. You can't drink from an empty cup. You won't be any good to others if you don't first take care of yourself. Lack of selfishness is the fastest route to turn us into bitter and ineffective team members, which is exactly the opposite of the Harmonizer's top priority.

Commit to developing your psychological and spiritual sides. Travel. Invest time in yourself. It's not always wise to put others first.

Logically, a Harmonizer knows the benefits of speaking up, and ironically, Harmonizers are often the ones that advocate and speak up for others.

Resistance to speak up, own your power, or take a stance typically comes from fear—fear that something will happen to you if you do. So get comfortable owning your voice and your story. You don't need to disguise what you want in deference to others' needs.

It's important to remember in interviewing that you have agency. That this is a two-way street. Your thoughts are valuable, and you are expected to voice your opinions. Harmonizers' complicated behavior doesn't always have the effect on others that they desire. They want to be seen as easygoing and low-maintenance, but it has the opposite effect in the long run. Gradually, as the person gets to know them they are continually let down and disappointed because they are not who they said they were. It is important to be very honest and vulnerable in the beginning of relationships, and interviewing is no exception. You may feel desperate and need a job, but eventually you will realize it's the wrong one for you.

How Harmonizers Can Manage Their Need to Fit In

Not every group and not every company is going to be a place where you will fit. Fitting in is great when it is a place that reflects your values and honors you. But to find that place you have to know *you.*

 INTERVIEW PRINCIPLE FOR JOB SEEKERS

> Not every group and not every company is going to be a place where you will fit. Fitting in is great when it is a place that reflects your values and honors you. But to find that place you have to know *you.*

Whereas Harmonizers are so focused on fitting in that they fail to consider if a role or company is a good fit for them, Challengers and Examiners do the opposite—they take the time to figure out if a role is a good fit before they get hired. They look at the interview as their opportunity to discover if it will be good for them. Charmers and Harmonizers do that *after* they get the job. They need the approval first, and once they isolate what the company or person wants from them, then they will think about the fit.

As a Harmonizer you can fit in anywhere, but once you gather some life experience you quickly realize that you need to be more choosy—it's not about just fitting in, it's about finding the right place to fit in! Before you begin interviewing, take some time to reflect on what it is you want. If you're a job seeker, outline the kind of company you want to work for and the role you want. If you're a hiring manager, write down what you want out of a candidate. Then ask someone you trust to hold you accountable after the interview as you consider whether the job or candidate aligns with the list you made.

I have worked with a CEO to help him hire for his lending business for over three years. He sees the best in everyone. He is a natural leader, and his employees love him; they would all run through walls for him. With this great power comes great responsibility. You see, he doesn't have a problem recruiting people to work for him, he has a problem making sure he chooses the *right* people. Because when you are generous and thoughtful and see the best in everyone, you think you can work with anyone. But building a business means creating a culture, and not just anyone will do. Your business requires certain employees to get the job done. Your industry, like his in finance, may require certain ethical standards, and if you don't ensure those are met in the hiring process you will have a mismatched culture that doesn't serve your clients. When Harmonizers interview well, it's because they recognize their own innate inability to be choosy. They know that they are just not the judgmental and critical type. So they need to create their own boundaries and requirements. My client decided to do this by creating his own mission and values for his company. He now asks himself if a candidate is honest, ethical, capable, and committed after every interview. While he still gets along great with everyone, he now has requirements for deciding the right one for the role. When Harmonizers interview well, it's because they have created limitations for themselves that don't come naturally to them. They know their natural tendency, and they are practiced at withholding and being more discerning to produce the results they need.

It is also helpful to acknowledge that the candidate, interviewer, or company culture is not perfect so that you do not idealize them. They don't have all the answers; they are just as flawed as you or I. When you approach a job or a company with this mindset, your need to contort yourself into an idealized version of yourself disappears.

When Harmonizers Interview Well

Harmonizers are warm and accepting. They generate a feeling of ease. They get to know you by listening and adding to what you have already said. Unlike other styles who put themselves out there, Harmonizers put the person they are speaking with on center stage. It's hard not to like someone who pays close attention to you the way a Harmonizer does.

Harmonizers are conscious that how they feel and what they think may change. They concede, they are willing to take the other person's view, they are very willing to give someone else credit, they are generous in goodwill. Challengers, their opposite, are more black and white, whereas Harmonizers are very at home in the gray areas. They know not everything is good or bad. They feel that they can't possibly get it right all the time; they are complex so they assume everyone else must be too. It is easy for them to see the nuance and take a balanced approach.

A Harmonizer who interviews well balances their need to fit in with an understanding of what they need. They do not forgo who they are; they know their limits and boundaries, and often that has come from experience ignoring their intuition in the past. Harmonizers are naturally great at making themselves easy to like, because they downplay any parts of their personality that may turn someone off. When a Harmonizer interviews well, they show their authentic self instead of a version that they think the person wants to see. A Harmonizer who opens up knows that it is disrespectful to themselves to pretend to be something they aren't.

When Harmonizers Interview Poorly

When a Harmonizer interviews poorly, it's often because they are overly relying on their ability to make themselves into what the other person wants. They lose themselves in trying to be what they think everyone else needs. Because you can never truly know what someone needs in an interview setting, by going in and acting in a way that you assume something can get you into trouble. You can come across as rudderless, indecisive, and ambivalent.

The fear that they will be rejected if they put themselves out there is so overwhelming that they sanitize themselves. They become watered down. This backfires because we need contrast. Harmonizers' fear of that and need to blend with others make it hard to see how they are different. An interviewer may leave the interaction thinking, *Who were they, what do they stand for, and what will I get?* A job seeker may leave the interaction unclear about what is expected of them in the role.

When Harmonizers interview poorly, they defer to the other person and devalue themselves, their experiences, and who they are, because they think it's more important that they get to know the other person.

This hurts others because you are not fairly representing yourself, or being honest with what you need. People need to know what you want so they can give it to you. If you don't tell them, they can't help you. People are stronger than you think; they can handle the truth. And they won't judge you as harshly as you judge yourself. And if that's not the case, you can walk away—the job wasn't meant for you. You can endure not being liked in the name of the truth or a cleansing conversation. This is a risk worth taking. Practice an inner resilience when you think that the worst might happen: you might not get the job, but you will find a different and perhaps even better one.

How to Interview a Harmonizer Job Seeker

Politeness is not what it used to be. In the past 150 years, the American culture has reinforced a more direct way of communicating, speaking your own mind, and being blunt. Politeness therefore became rude because politeness can seem insincere or fake. In the way that Charmers can be seen as chameleons, Harmonizers can be seen as too nice, which has its faults.

Harmonizers have a deliberate strategy to protect others. They take enormous amounts of energy to spare others from themselves. They think that who they are and what they think is probably not acceptable to most people, so therefore they need to keep it hidden.

Harmonizers are aware that others may be in very different situations than they are, and therefore they withhold their opinions or ideas to not ostracize them. They just never know what their audience really feels, and they are not willing to put themselves out there until they know. Their interview strategy is based on the understanding that there may be a huge difference between people and your views may not be their views. Unlike a Challenger, who assumes that most people have a very strong conviction like them, and if they say something it will make them spiral into self-doubt or self-criticism, a Harmonizer is always careful not to say anything that might push someone into an uncomfortable place because they themselves do not want to be asked to do anything uncomfortable, offer their own opinions, or put a stake in the ground.

Since a Harmonizer is concerned with how others feel, answering interview questions about themselves is an act of bravery. With little information, they have to put a stake in the ground and commit to a viewpoint or an opinion without first gathering all the evidence that they normally would before engaging in such vulnerability. Being who they are is easy with their close friends and family, but to do it in a boardroom with strangers feels almost rude and presumptuous.

To help a Harmonizer job seeker get past this barrier and open up, it's important that hiring managers create a safe place in the interview. This is key because a hiring manager who comes out swinging, challenging a Harmonizer job seeker, will only lead them to shut down, and you won't get an accurate or full picture of who they are or what they can do. Make them feel comfortable and encourage them to talk about themselves and own their successes. Convey that you invited them to interview because you believe they have what it takes. This will give them the confidence to be themselves. Saying things like "Tell me what you did," "We want to hear your opinion," or "How did you feel about that?" encourages them to speak from the first person and use *I* versus *we*. It pushes them to speak more concretely about themselves and their qualifications.

Harmonizers will never take the lead in conversations, so when you are interviewing them it is important to pull back on how much you speak. This is one of the best pieces of advice for all hiring managers—make sure you're speaking less than the interviewees—but it is especially important when interviewing Harmonizers. Ask deep questions and then open up the floor and give them room to talk. You'll hear more from them and leave the interview with a better sense of who they are.

 INTERVIEW PRINCIPLE FOR HIRING MANAGERS

Hiring managers should spend significantly less time talking in interviews than the candidates. You should focus on asking questions only and then giving ample space for the job seeker to answer, share about themselves, and prove why they are qualified.

How to Interview with a Harmonizer Hiring Manager

In the way that a Challenger hiring manager, the Harmonizer's opposite, approaches an interview like an intense cross-examination, Harmonizers approach interviews like a tryout for a team. Harmonizers embody the belief that everyone has value and their job as a hiring manager is to discover what that is. They don't approach an interview in the skeptical way a Challenger does, wanting to see if this person is really who they say they are. Harmonizers instead want to know who you are, and they want to give you a shot. An evolved and practiced Harmonizer knows that not everyone will have what it takes, but this knowledge often comes from years of having given people who don't have the skills a shot because when it comes down to it a Harmonizer never wants to be the one to say no or decide that a person isn't right—they believe that there is always something there that can be of value. In this way, these beliefs and traits make them incredible leaders, but they are not always the most discerning interviewers.

They don't talk very much, they listen more, and a job seeker may feel as though they are in a therapy session more than an interview. There is less "Tell me why you did this" and more "Why did that happen?" energy. Even though as a hiring manager the Harmonizer has all the power, they are never quite comfortable with that responsibility and would rather make the candidate comfortable and allow them to answer in their own way and in their own time. To job seekers, especially Challengers or Examiners, this might come across as not rigorous enough, like they're not really being interviewed. This is ironic, because the imperative to talk should be on a job seeker in an interview, not the hiring manager. It's good that they want to hear you talk.

Harmonizers often believe that they are being kind, understanding, and open-minded in their approach, but a job seeker may see it as wishy-washy, and therefore not feel secure in a decision to work for someone who comes across as noncommittal. As the job seeker, here is where you need to suspend your assumptions and skepticism and let go of how you think an interview should be conducted. To a Harmonizer, an interview only takes place if they feel that a candidate is capable; they don't need you to prove that in the interview. Trust that they are convinced of that aspect before the interview and allow them to get to know you more. Just because they approach interviews differently than you does not mean that they don't know how to do their job or would not be good to work with. Try to see the reason behind their approach and respect that it feels right to them.

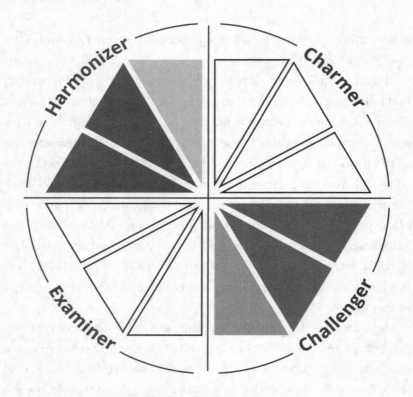

How a Harmonizer Interviews with Their Opposite—the Challenger

Challengers are task-focused and expressive, and their interview style is steadfast and doesn't change depending on the situation, whereas Harmonizers rely on their ability to connect, read the other person, and adapt accordingly. Harmonizers almost always defer to the other person to determine who will lead the conversation, but in this dynamic, they may feel as if they don't have a choice but to follow the Challenger's lead. Challengers will focus on a candidate's work product and motivations. They will want to examine a candidate's answers and get into the nitty-gritty, and this may be difficult for candidates because often Challengers don't balance that with an interest in who they are, leaving Harmonizers feeling that they have talked a lot about their skills but not much about the things they prioritize, like connecting, talking about what their team needs, and company culture. Challengers are all business; don't take it personally. They are impressed with preparation and focus. Harmonizers make people feel heard, which, along with being respected, is a priority of a Challenger. In that way, the conversation will feel natural.

How You Can Balance Your Approach and Tap into the Other Styles

Harmonizers can be more successful if they pull traits from other styles to balance out their natural tendencies:

- *Harmonizers can tap into the Charmers ability to own a room while also not rocking the boat.*
- *Harmonizers will perform better in an interview when they worry less about their audience and more about what they need in the way a Challenger does.*
- *Harmonizers can own their wants and needs by tapping into the Examiners steadfastness and unwavering commitment to themselves.*

Advice for Harmonizers	**Pre-interview Mantras for Harmonizers to Manage Their Need to Fit in**
It pays to own your own story.	"I can stand alone." "I advocate for myself."

Key Takeaways for Harmonizer Job Seekers

- Prioritizing others is admirable, but an interview is not about others, it's about you. You need to get comfortable selling yourself as an individual, not just as a coworker or team member. You don't need a team to show your value; you have value as an individual contributor.

- You withhold if you are unsure who your audience is. Get comfortable being yourself no matter who your audience is. Overly prioritizing others has you hyperaware of how you should present yourself to fit in.

Key Takeaways for Harmonizer Hiring Managers

- You will be attracted to a candidate's potential; fight this urge. You are not hiring someone's potential. Rather, you want to hire someone who has proven they can do the job through their past experience or how they explain their transferable skills in an interview.

- Your natural tendency is to allow someone to open up to you in their own way; however, an interview doesn't allow for that. You need to prepare interview questions that ask specifically how someone is qualified and why they want the job.

- Get comfortable with being uncomfortable. As the interviewer, you need to ask questions and let the candidate squirm—not easy for someone who is helpful.

PART III

APPLYING INTERVIEW STYLES

13

What I Discovered When I Discovered the Four Interview Styles

As I reflect on the first interview that changed my life, my college interview, I now know why I got in. You see, it wasn't the story I told, I didn't charm them, and it certainly wasn't my SAT scores. It wasn't that I was some interviewing savant, some natural who talked her way into an Ivy League school. It was that despite my shame and fear, I was myself. Warts and all. At the time I felt like it was my only option: I had to be myself and explain what I had been through to show them why they should admit me. I didn't have enough life experience to think of all the reasons why this approach might be a bad idea. It was the last time I was so unabashedly me in an interview. And as time goes on, I look back on that interview as a high watermark.

Despite years of research and now knowing so much more about how people interview, the truth is, I knew the answer all along. The key to interviewing better isn't out there somewhere. It's not perfect answers memorized, the perfect resume, or the perfect suit. You already have it within you. It's *you*!

We all have it within us to be ourselves, yet life and jobs and relationships tell us otherwise. We get in our heads. We listen to the wrong people, consume toxic content, and self-doubt creeps in. We compare ourselves to the competition, imaginary or real. We make bets against ourselves. We wonder why anyone would admit us, hire us, or promote us. We get so deep in our heads that we build anxiety that can feel insurmountable. As a coping mechanism, we relegate interviewing to this thing that is not that important. Or we tell ourselves that we can't do it and we are bad at it.

We start to think we are bad at it because we are not sure who we should be in an interview. And that's because there is no one way to be; there is no standard interview. So we are left questioning ourselves and how best to sell ourselves in a situation that feels ambiguous.

In discovering interview styles, I learned that we all have a story and a background. Some of our stories are sad and tragic. Others are average or even great. It's not our story that defines us, but what we do with it. Who we become because of it. How we take what we have been given and make it into something we want. We all have something that we have to learn to live with, but the degrees are not the same and the opportunities are not the same for everyone. I can't take my childhood trauma away, but I can mine my despair for lessons. We must ask ourselves, *How has it made me who I am, and what the hell am I going to do with it?*

In helping thousands of clients, I've learned what makes people successful, especially in interviews. People get where they want to go when they know where they want to go. That is it. Knowing what *you* want and where *you* want to go is the best way to decrease ambiguity. It's the way to end up where you want.

All those years ago, I knew what I wanted. I wanted to get into a great school to change my life. I accomplished that, and it was because I was single-minded, driven, and sure of myself. That knowing doesn't come out of nowhere; it comes from knowing oneself, one's preferences, goals, and ambitions. It certainly doesn't come from friends, social media, or your parents. Knowing oneself is an inside job. Believing that someone else will give you insight into you, that the solution lies outside of you, and that you are not enough diminishes the power of your own voice, your own story, and what you want.

In our society we are bombarded with messages that we are not enough, that we should be doing more or doing things differently. Consumerism and comparison is a trap to make you believe that you are not good enough. That you must buy something or go somewhere, that happiness is somewhere over the rainbow. That the way you do things isn't right. I am here to tell you that you are enough as you are. All you need is a knowledge of your own power and how to access it.

I hope that discovering your interview style has empowered you. I hope that by reading all these stories you are feeling confident to tell your own story.

I hope you know now that how you do it is just as important as what you do. I hope you learned from Mike how important it is to know what you want. I hope you learned from Julia that practicing and preparing is half the battle. I hope Steve inspired you to dig deep and access parts of yourself that you might bury. I hope Anita reminded you to not get carried away with the things that you are "supposed" to want, but to connect with what you need.

I hope that insight into your style and the styles of others can show you where your assumptions are wrong. Where you've dismissed others who represent things you don't identify with. That you use knowledge of your style as a mirror to show you where you could do better, and knowledge of the other styles to show you how.

This is what I hope for everyone who reads this book and discovers their interview style: that it compels you to reflect. Where do you rely on shortcuts and biases? Where have you created beliefs that your way is the right way? Perhaps you are a Challenger, and you believe that if someone is quiet in interviews they mustn't be interested. Perhaps you're an Examiner and see sharing stories about yourself as bragging and think those who do it are smarmy. If you're a Harmonizer and the priority to adapt to the company is paramount, those who are more self-involved might rub you the wrong way. Or maybe you're a Charmer and simply don't "get" anyone who won't connect.

What if Charmers borrowed the self-assuredness of being steadfast? What if Challengers could tame the need to be right and adapt the way a Harmonizer does? What if an Examiner opened up and enjoyed the process the way a Charmer relishes an interview? What if we all softened our approach a bit to balance out our style, taking the best from each of the four styles?

Mike, Julia, Steve, and Anita allowed me to discover a better part of myself. I learned the areas where I excel and where I have my limits. I now consciously tap into my opposite and imagine what my opposite would do. It's helped me discover ways to be more empathetic and more myself. Most importantly, I discovered care and compassion for others that come from a deep appreciation for who they are, not who I want them to be.

Acknowledgments

To my followers: this book wouldn't have been possible without you.

To Mike, Julia, Steve, and Anita. You know who you are. Thank you for letting me share your stories; they will surely help a lot of people.

To all the individuals I have worked with since 2011. Although I don't name every one of you, in helping you, I learned so much. This book is a result of thousands of coaching hours, thousands of resume reviews, thousands of interviews, and hundreds of training sessions. I wouldn't know what I know if you hadn't trusted me to help you, and in turn I created this to help many more.

To my children, who taught me how to see and appreciate differences and love so completely—everything I do, I do for you. You are my greatest accomplishment. And to Aaron, for encouraging me to share my story with the world.

Thank you to Arlene and Don for being my first fans and to the Lewes crew, especially Fred and Linda, for helping me navigate the publishing world and being there for me at the very beginning and telling me to "write it all."

To the people who love me so much that it has taught me how to love myself and see my own best qualities while they lovingly tolerate my bad qualities. Daniel, the most charming person I have ever known, you remind me every day where I came from, you never let me forget where I am going, and you make the whole ride so much fun. Yael, who taught me all those years ago to stop thinking so much, to trust the process and just do it. Deirdre, my fellow navel gazer, you were the first to see the value of this idea, and I continue to return to your support year after year because you hold special my sacred intention. Eric, thank you for believing in me and encouraging me. To Aunt Lynda, who embodies enthusiasm and lives life with the curiosity of a child, I am in awe of you. To Aunt Patty, for teaching me that I had the power all along, you are my Glinda the Good Witch and have always been my inspiration.

May this book be a continuation of my grandparents' memory and legacy. To Miguel: losing you forever changed me.

To the original four interview styles, David, Anuj, Zack, and Nicolino. I'll never forget our whiteboard sessions and philosophical conversations on campus while eating bad pizza, crepes, and chicken from a truck.

To Sarah and Becky, thank you being some of the first to take "my baby," the Interviewology Profile, and teach it with the same level of professionalism, enthusiasm, and passion that I do. Forever grateful. To my team of mock interviewers and trainers: Russell, Veronica, and Kevin.

To Deb, you were the perfect boss and there is no doubt that I am here and that I do what I do because you saw it in me and therefore helped me see it in myself. To the Bonnie's, what a great team we made at CS&B.

To my corporate clients, who see the value in my product and trainings. To my university clients, especially Temple University, where I got my start and conducted my research, and to all the schools across the country that use Interviewology Profile now.

To the people who help me write better, Kirby and Hollis at HarperCollins. Ours was a very cocreative, supportive relationship that any author would kill to have, and you spoiled me so much on my first book that I fear you've ruined me forever. To Stacey Glick, my agent, and Danielle Dupré, my research assistant. To my beta readers, Nicole, Sarah, Bianca, Michelle, and Robin. Without you I would still be wondering if I got my message across the way I intended. Each one of you gave me incredible insights, support, and help while writing for which this book and I are better because of you. Especially to Robin, the genius behind the name Interviewology.

To the data scientists at Assessment Standards Institute, Dr. Dennis Koerner and Dr. Russ Watson: thank you for your guidance, wisdom, and accountability.

I stand on the shoulders of the authors whom I quote and the researchers who came before me. I couldn't have had these insights or accomplished any of this without their efforts, and for that I am forever indebted to the work that came before mine.

To Sam Wood, my graphic designer, who takes my ideas and makes them beautiful. To my business development associates, marketing team, website gurus, and social media mavens: I couldn't do what I do without you.

And most of all I acknowledge you: thank you for reading this book! Thank you for wanting to get better at interviewing, and thank you for letting me be the person that gets to help you on this incredibly important part of your journey. I always say to all my clients at the end of sessions, this is the hardest part, it gets better, and until it does, I am here holding a space for you on the other side. I believe in you. Good luck!

Deciphering the Interview Styles

R ead these snippets of real interviews. Can you identify the interview style?

Tyronne, recruiter for a large nonprofit, conducting a phone
screen for an IT position

TYRONNE: "Hi, is this still a good time to talk?"

CANDIDATE: "Absolutely, I've been looking forward to meeting
you and getting to know more about the job."

TYRONNE: "Okay."

Awkward silence

TYRONNE: "Why do you want to leave your current job? Why do
you want to work here?"

CANDIDATE: "Well, as you can see on my resume I have been
with my current company for eleven years, and I feel it's a great
time for me to move on. I am looking for a new challenge, and
I see that this job—I read the job description on your website, it
says that you need someone to manage your new cybersecurity
software. I am really passionate about cybersecurity, and I excel
at taking the lead on projects. In fact, my most recent project
was spearheading a new accounting software and deploying it

company wide. It was a big success! There are so many moving parts to getting everyone on board to making sure there aren't any bugs/issues, and then you have all the updates. I consider myself a natural leader. I think my coworkers would agree. I wish you could've seen my coworkers' faces when I told them we had to work overnight to deploy the new software, but it was all good—I bought everyone pizza."

TYRONNE: "Ummm, you wouldn't have to work at night here. It's a traditional nine-to-five position."

CANDIDATE: "Oh yeah, of course, but I will go above and beyond, ya know. That's just, like, how I do it. With my kids, for example, I pack their lunches every day, and I make sure to be at every practice. I even coach all their teams. Last year my son's Little League team made it to the playoffs. Do you play sports?"

TYRONNE: "I did a little in college . . . but back to . . ."

CANDIDATE: "Me too. Played softball and football. Man, football is so dangerous nowadays, though, not sure I want my kids playing it. Do you have kids?"

TYRONNE: "No, I am not married. Let's get back on track . . ."

Answer

Tyronne, the hiring manager, is an Examiner. He doesn't make small talk, but he engages in formalities, like checking in to make sure he is ready, and then jumps right into interview questions. Like diving into the deep end.

The candidate is a Charmer, a little taken aback when the interview starts without any small talk. He is complimentary and talks about his experience using stories and tries to connect personally. However, Tyronne, an Examiner, doesn't bite. He keeps it very professional and doesn't give the candidate any indication if he is doing well or poorly in his eyes.

In this scenario, the candidate may leave the interaction feeling confused. His usual tactic of asking personal questions to get to know the person didn't work. He got nowhere. He will most likely think he did well and the hiring manager was just busy.

Tyronne will be annoyed by this interaction. He would've liked the candidate to keep his answers short, to the point, focused on just his experience and how he is qualified for the job, how his skills match the job description. He left the interaction thinking he wouldn't mind working with him but not knowing if he could do the job, so he's going to pass on the candidate in favor of candidates who give him a better sense of their ability to do the job.

Scenario 2:

Deb, an HR director, conducting a second-round interview for an HR generalist position in her department

DEB: "Thanks so much for coming in today. Let me tell you a little bit about the role, the company, and the team you will be working with. I have led this department for eleven years. Prior to this I came over from UPS. I was there for eight years. It was an intense workplace, with unions and lots of regulations. We pitched in and had to be able to work in the distribution facility and do every job in the building should there be a strike. I learned a lot there. Here, it's a different animal. Going from transportation and shipping to insurance was big a change for me. My biggest responsibilities are managing the benefits, employee relations issues, and our recruiting efforts. As you know we need an HR generalist to help us with benefits, employee relations, and payroll. I read your resume, and I know you are currently working at Comcast as a generalist. I am familiar with the company. What HR software do you use at Comcast?"

CANDIDATE: "We use the xyz software."

DEB: "Oh, interesting, that's great, that is what we use. Can you tell me how to make an employee change and how you run payroll?"

CANDIDATE: "Yes. We would first create a new ticket and fill out the information and save the—"

DEB: Without letting the candidate finish, "Right, exactly. How about payroll?"

CANDIDATE: "Well, I am not so sure about that. Which part of the process are you referring to?"

DEB: "For us, we use Paycheck and it's a three-part process. And we get the reports ready in Excel. How familiar are you with Excel? Do you know pivot tables?"

CANDIDATE: "No, I am sorry, I don't."

Answer

Deb is a Challenger. She talks a lot. Tells the candidate a lot about herself and then peppers her with questions. Without any small talk or rapport building, the candidate feels as if they are in an interrogation.

The candidate is a Harmonizer. Listens attentively, doesn't try to interrupt or interject her thoughts or opinions or ask questions. She feels as though it isn't her place to rock the boat since this person is in the position of power. She thinks, *If this interviewer wants to talk the whole time, I will listen.*

Deb thinks she has to carry the conversion because she's in charge, but that leads her to cut off the candidate and interrupt. The candidate thinks they are doing a bad job and withholds further. The push and pull of this dynamic is off. The Challenger is too much for the timid Harmonizer.

The Four Interview Styles

HARMONIZER

Harmonizer/ Examiner   Harmonizer   Harmonizer/ Charmer

"I want to adapt."

- Empathetic
- Collaborator
- Observant
- Warm
- Accepting
- Easy going

CHARMER

Charmer/ Harmonizer   Charmer   Charmer/ Challenger

"I want to be liked."

- Enthusiastic
- Engaging
- Approval seeking
- Confident
- Willing
- Personable

Accomodating

Introvert   Extrovert

- Cautious
- Deliberate
- Stable
- Reliable
- Private
- Knowledgable

"I want to get it right."

Examiner/ Harmonizer   Examiner   Examiner/ Challenger

EXAMINER

Steadfast

- Thought provoking
- Truthful
- Undaunted
- Determined
- Strong
- Passionate

"I want to be me."

Challenger/ Examiner   Challenger   Challenger/ Charmer

CHALLENGER

Interview Style Cheat Sheet

F ollowing is a cheat sheet to the four interview styles, a quick breakdown of the main takeaways for each style. Refer back to this list for a refresher whenever you need.

What Each Style Prioritizes

Charmer "I want to be liked." Seek approval/Fear not being accepted or liked

Challenger "I want to be me/heard." Want to be heard/Fear not being respected

Examiner "I want to get it right." Fear of being vulnerable

Harmonizer "I want to adapt/fit in." Fear of not belonging

How Each Style Shows Their Value

Charmers show their value by being eager.

Challengers show their value by questioning.

Examiners show their value by being precise.

Harmonizers show their value by being agreeable.

How Each Style Sees Interviews

Charmers see interviews as a performance (on a stage)

Challengers see interviews as an investigation (cross-examination in a courtroom)

Examiners see interviews as a test (that will be graded)

Harmonizers see interviews as a tryout (for a team)

Advice for Each Style

Charmer: It pays to be yourself.

Challenger: It pays to trust.

Examiner: It pays to connect.

Harmonizer: It pays to own your story.

Each Style at Their Worst

Charmers coerce

Challengers demand

Harmonizers downplay

Examiners withhold

What Each Style Focuses On

Charmers and **Harmonizers** focus on other people, externally

Challengers and **Examiners** focus on themselves, internally

What Is Important to Each Style

Charmers and **Challengers:** The past is important; let's talk about the future.

Harmonizers and **Examiners:** The past is irrelevant; let's talk about the present.

What Each Style Is Drawn To

Charmers find people who like them.

Challengers are good at finding people who will be great subordinates.

Examiners are adept at finding the *i* dotters and *t* crossers.

Harmonizers are drawn to potential.

List of Universal Truths, Myths, and Interview Principles

Universal Truths

- You can't choose your interview style, the same way you can't choose your personality.

- We all have a tendency to think that everyone interviews the way we do and that our way is the best way.

- Each style has variations and learning curves. When you are at your best, you are balancing your traits and shifting your approach for those you are interviewing with.

- We like to interview with people who are like us.

- Opposite interview styles are a great place to look for traits to draw on to balance your overused strengths.

Universal Myths

- There's a right way and a wrong way to interview.

- Telling someone what they want to hear will get you the job.

- An interview isn't something you can prepare for; you'll do better on the spot because you'll sound scripted if you prepare.

- If you've done poorly in interviews before, you're bad at interviewing.

Interview Principles for Job Seekers

- The act of creating a resume, thinking about your work experience, and practicing answers to interview questions can help build your self-awareness and confidence. Doing so can help you interview better.

- Use the STAR method to create answers to common behavioral questions.

  ° **Situation:** Describe the situation you were in or a task that you needed to accomplish. Use a real-life example from a job, class, or volunteer experience and be specific.

  ° **Task:** Clearly define the goal you were working toward in that situation.

  ° **Action:** The interviewer wants to hear what *you* did. Use the word *I*, along with powerful action words.

  ° **Result:** Describe what happened and how you were responsible for it. This is your time to shine! The story should showcase how you were the hero—how you retained the tough customer, or finished the project ahead of schedule, or saved the company $40,000. Most of the time, candidates leave the interviewer hanging, so always give the result without having to be asked. Don't be shy! An interview is the time and place to talk about your successes.

  ° If you have a tendency to talk too much (or not enough), then this formula will keep you on track.

  ° For an interviewer, using the STAR method means asking about specific situations using behavioral questions like, "Describe a situation in which you were able to use persuasion to successfully convince someone to see things your way," and "Step by step, using a real-life example, please tell me how you delegated responsibilities on a project and how a candidate handled it."

- Hiring managers and HR people are not trained to give you feedback on your interview. If you need feedback, it's best to hire a coach who can work with you to improve.

- Active listening is key to show your interviewer you are engaged. Make eye contact as they speak, nod your head, and make occasional agreeing sounds.

- Ask the right people the right questions. Ask HR people questions about company culture and next steps in the interview process. Save questions about the job and where it will lead for the hiring manager.

- Record yourself as you practice answering interview questions. Seeing yourself from another perspective can help show you where you have room for improvement.

- You aren't bad at interviewing; you are just unprepared.

- It isn't helpful to spend time focusing on your competition. There's no way to prove that your assumptions about them are correct, and you waste precious time thinking about others when you should be building your own self-awareness. Your best bet is not to know your competition, but to know yourself and be able to convey clearly who you are.

- Taking time to answer makes a better impression; you come across as thoughtful as opposed to rushing and talking fast.

- All jobs are valuable, and you will be more confident when you look at your experience without criticism. Updating your resume is a good exercise to building an appreciation for your past roles. If you can reflect objectively on your experience, you can reflect on all that you've done and begin to make connections to where you're hoping to go.

- An interview is not just about getting a job. It can also be an exercise in learning what you want for your career. Just as you notice things you like during an interview, pay attention to things that you don't like—aspects of the role, qualities of the hiring manager, or details related to the company culture. These will help inform your decisions and help you eventually end up in the job that is right for you.

- You can't sell yourself if you don't tell someone *who* you are— you are the most important part of your story.

- Not every group and not every company is going to be a place where you will fit. Fitting in is great when it is a place that reflects your values and honors you. But to find that place, you have to know *you*.

Interview Principles for Hiring Managers

- Our first impressions are often wrong, and someone's performance in an interview is not always a good indicator of whether or not they can do the job.

- If the gatekeepers are handpicking people and positively reinforcing certain behaviors from a place of bias, they will create organizations that are skewed and populations that don't represent society but represent their biases.

- Structured interviews, where you ask the same questions of each candidate, are a great way to decrease bias in the interview process.

- Hiring managers have less experience than job seekers and 90 percent are untrained to interview. You are *not* bad at interviewing; you're just unprepared.

- Often, we conduct social interviews, which are closer to conversations. Behavioral interviews can decrease ambiguity, and are more effective and less biased.

- Hiring managers should spend significantly less time talking in interviews than the candidates. You should focus on asking questions only and then giving ample space for the job seeker to answer, share about themselves, and prove why they are qualified.

Notes

2 HOW I DISCOVERED THE FOUR INTERVIEW STYLES

18   Learning styles: Howard Gardner, *Frames of Mind: The Theory of Multiple Intelligences* (New York: Basic Books, 1943–1983).

24   As of April 2020: Dennis Koerner to Anna Papalia, Memphis, TN, April 9, 2020.

24   data reliability: Data reliability, often assessed using Cronbach's Alpha, is a statistical measure used to evaluate the internal consistency and reliability of a psychometric assessment or test. A high Cronbach's Alpha value suggests that the assessment is more reliable, while a low value may indicate inconsistencies in the assessment's items. Construct validity refers to the degree to which a particular assessment accurately measures the theoretical construct it is designed to assess. Establishing construct validity ensures that the assessment provides accurate and meaningful results, and it involves empirical and theoretical evidence to support its claims. Disparate impact is a concept used in the evaluation of assessments to identify potential discrimination or bias against certain groups. It refers to a situation where a particular assessment has a disproportionately negative impact on the performance of individuals from a specific demographic group (e.g., based on race, gender, ethnicity, or other protected characteristics). Dennis W. Koerner and Russell J. Watson. Assessment Selection Standards Guide. Assessment Standards Institute. 2020.

3 WHY IT'S IMPORTANT TO KNOW YOUR INTERVIEW STYLE

27   and it is expected: R. Mauer, "The Pros and Cons of Virtual and In-Person Interviews," Society for Human Resource Management, March 26, 2021, retrieved March 12, 2023, from https://www.shrm.org/resourcesandtools/hr-topics/talent-acquisition/pages/pros-and-cons-virtual-in-person-interviews.aspx.

27   The wrong hires: David Pedulla, *Making the Cut: Hiring Decisions, Bias, and the Consequences of Nonstandard, Mismatched, and Precarious Employment* (Princeton, NJ: Princeton University Press, 2020).

29   As shown by researchers like David S. Pedulla: Pedulla, *Making the Cut.*

29   Our organizations: A. J. Hillman, A. A. Cannella, and I. C., "Women and Racial Minorities in the Boardroom: How Do Directors Differ?," *Journal of Management* 28, no. 6 (2002): 747–63, DOI: 10.1177/014920630202800603; Stephanie B. Smith, "Overcoming the race-sex barrier: what matters most in the executive sponsorship of black women," *College of Business Theses and Dissertations* 11 (2019), https://via.library.depaul.edu/business_etd/11/; Juliana Menasce Horowitz, Anna Brown, and Kiana Cox, "Race in America 2019," Pew Research Center, April 9, 2019, https://www.pewsocialtrends.org/2019/04/09/race-in-america-2019; Griffin Sims Edwards; digitalundivided's ProjectDiane 2018.

29   If the gatekeepers: Louis Lippens, Siel Vermeiren, and Stijn Baert, "The State of Hiring Discrimination: A Meta-Analysis of (Almost) all Recent Correspondence Experiments," *European Economic Review* 151 (2023), DOI: 10.1016/j.eurecorev.2022.104315.

30   Pragya Agarwal: Emily Kwong, "Understanding Unconscious Bias," July 15, 2020, in *Short Wave*, podcast, https://www.npr.org/2020/07/14/891140598/understanding-unconscious-bias; Pragya Agarwal, *Sway: Unraveling Unconscious Bias* (New York, NY: Bloomsbury Sigma, 2020).

32   They found: Marianne Bertrand and Sendhil Mullainathan, "Are Emily and Greg More Employable Than Lakisha and Jamal? A Field Experiment on Labor Market Discrimination," *American Economic Review* 94, no. 4 (2004): 992, DOI: 10.1257/0002828042002561.

33   the likelihood: The Prison Policy Initiative, "Out of Prison & Out of Work: Unemployment Among Formerly Incarcerated People," July 2018, https://www.prisonpolicy.org/reports/outofwork.html; U.S. Department of Justice Office of Justice Programs and Bureau of Justice, "Employment of Persons Released from Federal Prison in 2010," December 2021, https://bjs.ojp.gov/content/pub/pdf/eprfp10.pdf.

34   some studies report: Tasha Eurich, *Insight: Why We're Not as Self-Aware as We Think, and How Seeing Ourselves Clearly Helps Us Succeed at Work and in Life* (Redfern, Australia: Currency Press, 2017).

34   Tasha Eurich: Tasha Eurich, "What Self-Awareness Really Is (and How to Cultivate It)," *Harvard Business Review*, January 4, 2018, https://hbsp.harvard.edu/product/H042DK-PDF-ENG?itemFindingMethod=Search.

37   Estimates: Adam Uzialko, "How Much Is That Bad Hire Really Costing Your Business?" *Business News Daily* (Waltham, MA), February 21, 2023, https://www.businessnewsdaily.com/9066-cost-of-bad-hire.html.

37   the halo effect: Gabrieli Giulio, Albert Lee, Peipei Setoh, and Gianluca Esposito, "An Analysis of the Generalizability and Stability of the Halo Effect During the COVID-19 Pandemic Outbreak," *Frontiers in Psychology* 12 (2021), DOI: 10.3389/fpsyg.2021.631871.

37   "like me effect": G. J. Sears and P. M. Rowe, "A personality-based similar-to-me effect in the employment interview: Conscientiousness, affect-versus competence-mediated interpretations, and the role of job relevance," *Canadian Journal of Behavioural Science/Revue canadienne des sciences du comportement*, 35, no. 1 (2003): 13–24, DOI: 10.1037/h0087182.

38   This is key: Greg Ashley and Roni Reiter-Palmon, "Self-awareness and the evolution of leaders: The need for a better measure of self-awareness," *Journal of Behavioral and Applied Management* 14 (2012): 2–17, DOI: 10.1037/t29152-000.

38   Studies show: Fabio Sala, "Executive Blind Spots: Discrepancies Between Self- and Other-Ratings," *Consulting Psychology Journal: Practice and Research* 55, no. 4 (2003): 222–29, DOI: 10.1037/1061-4087.55.4.222.

38   The average job seeker: Zippia, "15+ Incredible Job Search Statistics [2023]: What Job Seekers Need To Know," Zippia.com, February 27, 2023, https://www.zippia.com/advice/job-search-statistics/.

39 Research shows that: A. G. Greenwald D. E. McGhee, and J. K. L. Schwartz, "Measuring Individual Differences in Implicit Cognition: The Implicit Association Test," *Journal of Personality and Social Psychology* 74 (1998): 1464–80, DOI: 10.1037/0022-3514.74.6.1464.

40 What we know: S. M. Ruzycki and S. B. Ahmed, "Equity, diversity and inclusion are foundational research skills," *Nature of Human Behavior* 6 (2022): 910–12, DOI: 10.1038/s41562-022-01406-7.

40 In an interview: "Interview with psychologist Anthony Greenwald," *PBS News-Hour*, PBS, 2020; Anthony G. Greenwald and Linda Hamilton Krieger, "Implicit Bias: Scientific Foundations," *California Law Review* 94, no. 4 (2006): 925–67, DOI: 10.2307/20439056.

42 75 percent: Alison Green, "Your Job Application Was Rejected by a Human, Not a Computer," *Ask a Manager*, October 13, 2020, https://www.askamanager.org/2020/10/your-job-application-was-rejected-by-a-human-not-a-computer.html.

4 THE FOUR INTERVIEW STYLES

51 This self-awareness: R. C. Smith, A. M. Dorsey, J. S. Lyles, and R. M. Frankel, "Teaching self-awareness enhances learning about patient-centered interviewing," *Academic Medicine* 74, no. 11 (1999): 1242–48, DOI: 10.1097/00001888-199911000-00020; J. Carden, R. J. Jones, and J. Passmore, "Defining Self-Awareness in the Context of Adult Development: A Systematic Literature Review," *Journal of Management Education* 46 (2022): 140–77, DOI: 10.1177/1052562921990065.

52 unlike a Myers-Briggs: Ken Randall, Mart Isaacson, and Carrie Ciro, "Validity and Reliability of the Myers-Briggs Personality Type Indicator: A Systematic Review and Meta-Analysis," *Journal of Best Practices in Health Professions Diversity* 10 (2017): 1–27, https://www.jstor.org/stable/26554264.

54 Mary Steffel: T. Eyal, M. Steffel, and N. Epley, "Perspective mistaking: Accurately understanding the mind of another requires getting perspective, not taking perspective," *Journal of Personality and Social Psychology* 114, no. 4 (2018): 547–71, DOI: 10.1037/pspa0000115.

5 CHARMER

66 describes Charmers: Robert Greene, *The Art of Seduction* (New York, NY: Penguin Books, 2003).

6 INTERVIEWING WITH A CHARMER

77 Charmers are accommodating: Francesca Gino, Ovul Sezer, and Laura Huang, "To be or not to be your authentic self? Catering to others' preferences hinders performance," *Organizational Behavior and Human Decision Processes* 158 (June 2020): 83–100, DOI: 10.1016/j.obhdp.2020.01.003.

78 Even though: Louise Archer, "Younger Academics' Constructions of 'authenticity,' 'success' and professional Identity," *Studies in Higher Education* 33, no. 4 (2008): 385–403, DOI: 10.1080/03075070802211729.

83 We want to open up: Zachary G. Baker, Reese Y. W. Tou, Jennifer L. Bryan, C. Raymond Knee, "Authenticity and Well-Being: Exploring Positivity and Negativity in Interactions as a Mediator, Personality and Individual Differences," *ScienceDirect*, 2017; 113, 235–39, DOI: 10.1016/j.pID.2017.03.018.

87 Charmers prefer: Julia Levashina, Christopher J. Hartwell, Frederick P. Morgeson, and Michael A. Campion, "The Structured Employment Interview: Narrative and Quantitative Review of the Research Literature," *Personnel Psychology* 67, no. 167 (2014): 241–93, DOI: 10.1111/peps.12052.

7 CHALLENGER

96 If you can't: Dave Zielinski, "Study: Most Job Seekers Abandon Online Job Applications," *Society for Human Resource Management*, March 8, 2016, https://www.shrm.org/resourcesandtools/hr-topics/technology/pages/study-most-job-seekers-abandon-online-job-applications.aspx.

97 Challengers understand: T.-Y. Kim, E. M. David, T. Chen, and Y. Liang, "Authenticity or Self-Enhancement? Effects of Self-Presentation and Authentic Leadership on Trust and Performance," *Journal of Management* 49, no. 3 (2023): 944–73, DOI: 10.1177/01492063211063807.

104 As is stated in StrengthsFinder: Don Clifton, StrengthsFinder 2.0, edited by Gallup. Gallup Press, 2007: 1.

9 EXAMINER

127 groundbreaking book: Daniel Goleman, *Emotional Intelligence: Why It Can Matter More Than IQ* (New York, NY: Random House Publishing Group, 2005), 143.

127 Goleman calls: Ibid., 144.

127 Goleman goes on to say: Ibid., 143.

128 capacity to be: Ibid., 144.

137 In Michaela Chung's book: Michaela Chung, *The Irresistible Introvert: Harness the Power of Quiet Charisma in a Loud World* (New York, NY: Skyhorse Publishing, 2016).

138 bias for extroverts: Ibid., 129.

138 As Chung goes on to say: Ibid., 62.

139 study in reciprocity: J. Eldridge, M. John, and K. Gleeson, "Confiding in others: exploring the experiences of young people who have been in care," *Adoption & Fostering* 44, no. 2 (2020): 156–72, DOI: 10.1177/0308575920920389; G. Cornelissen S. Dewitte, L. Warlop, "Are social value orientations expressed automatically? Decision making in the dictator game," *Personality & Social Psychology Bulletin* 37, no. 8 (2011): 1080–90, DOI: 10.1177/0146167211405996.

10 INTERVIEWING WITH AN EXAMINER

150 he illustrates: Nicholas Epley, *Mindwise: Why We Misunderstand What Others Think, Believe, Feel, and Want* (New York, NY: Vintage Publishing, 2015), 105, 300.

151 Ellen Hendriksen, PhD, calls: Ellen Hendriksen, *How to Be Yourself: Quiet Your Inner Critic and Rise Above Social Anxiety* (New York, NY: St. Martin's Press, 2018).

153 Martha Beck said it best: Marth Beck, *Finding Your Own North Star: Claiming the Life You Were Meant to Live* (Easton, PA: Harmony Press, 2002), 179.

CHAPTER 11: HARMONIZER

170 Harmonizers believe: Matthew T. Gailliot, Roy F. Baumeister, "Self-esteem, belongingness, and worldview validation: Does belongingness exert a unique influence upon self-esteem?" *Journal of Research in Personality* 41, no. 2 (2007): 327–45, DOI: 10.1016/j.jrp.2006.04.004.

CHAPTER 12: INTERVIEWING WITH A HARMONIZER

186 explains confidence: Meg Jay, *The Defining Decade: Why your Twenties matter—and how to make the most of them now* (New York, NY: Twelve Books, 2012), 12.

186 significant amount of research: Cornelissen et al., "Are social value orientations expressed automatically?" 1080–90.

Additional References

Bonnefon, Jean-Francois, Aidan Feeney, Wim De Neys. "The Risk of Polite Misunderstandings." *Current Directions in Psychological Science* 20 (2011): 321–24. DOI: 10.1177/0963721411418472.

Bye, Hege, J. Horverak, Gro Sandal, David Sam, and Fons Van de Vijver. "Cultural fit and ethnic background in the job interview." *International Journal of Cross Cultural Management* 14 (2013): 7–26. DOI: 10.1177/1470595813491237.

Carden, J., R. J. Jones, and J. Passmore. "Defining Self-Awareness in the Context of Adult Development: A Systematic Literature Review." *Journal of Management Education* 46, no.1 (2022): 140–77. DOI: 10.1177/1052562921990065.

Cohen, D., and J. P. Schmidt. "Ambiversion: Characteristics of Midrange Responders on the Introversion-Extraversion Continuum." *Journal of Personality Assessment* 43, no. 5 (1979): 514–16. DOI: 10.1207/s15327752jpa4305_14.

Constantin, Kaytlin, Deborah Powell, and Julie McCarthy. "Expanding conceptual understanding of interview anxiety and performance: Integrating cognitive, behavioral, and physiological features." *International Journal of Selection and Assessment* 29, no. 2 (2021): 234–52. DOI: 10.1111/ijsa.12326.

Dasen, P. "Culture and Cognitive Development From a Piagetian Perspective." In *Psychology and Culture*, edited by W. J. Lonner and R. S. Malpass (1993): 145–49.

Dillahunt, Tawanna R., Lucas Siqueira Rodrigues, Joey Chiao-Yin Hsiao, and Mauro Cherubini. "Self-regulation and Autonomy in the Job Search: Key Factors to Support Job Search Among Swiss Job Seekers." *Interacting with Computers* 33, no. 5 (September 2021): 537–63. DOI: 10.1093/iwc/iwac008.

Donato, A. A., R. L. Alweis, and C. Fitzpatrick. "Rater perceptions of bias using the Multiple Mini-Interview format: a qualitative study." *Journal of Education and Training Studies* 3, no. 5 (2015): 52–58. DOI: 10.11114/jets.v3i5.818.

Duckworth, Angela, Christopher Peterson, Michael Matthews, and Dennis Kelly. "Grit: Perseverance and Passion for Long-Term Goals." *Journal of Personality and Social Psychology* 92 (2007): 1087–1101. DOI: 10.1037/0022-3514.92.6.1087.

Engelhardt, P. E., J. T. Nigg, and F. Ferreira. "Is the Fluency of Language Outputs Related to Individual Differences in Intelligence and Executive Function?" *Acta Psychologica* 144, no. 2 (2013): 424–32. DOI: 10.1016/j.actpsy.2013.08.002.

Freeman, R. Edward, and Ellen R. Auster. "Values, Authenticity, and Responsible Leadership." *Journal of Business Ethics* 98 (2011): 15–23. DOI: 10.1007/s10551-011-1022-7.

Gino, Francesca, Ovul Sezer, and Laura Huang. "To Be or Not to Be Your Authentic self? Catering to Others' Preferences Hinders Performance." *ScienceDirect* 158 (2020): 83–100. DOI: 10.1016/j.obhdp.2020.01.003.

Higgins, Chad A., and Timothy A. Judge. "The Effect of Applicant Influence Tactics on Recruiter Perceptions of Fit and Hiring Recommendations: A Field Study." *Journal of Applied Psychology* 89, no. 4 (2004): 622–32. DOI: 10.1037/0021-9010.89.4.622.

Judge, Timothy A., Chad A Higgins, and Daniel M. Cable. "The Employment Interview: A Review of Recent Research and Recommendations for Future Research." *Human Resources Management Review* 10, no. 4 (2000): 383–406. https://today.iit.edu/wp-content/uploads/2015/03/Judge-Higgins-Cable-.pdf.

Kahneman, D., P. Slovic, and A. Tversky, eds. "Judgement Under Uncertainty: Heuristics and Biases." Cambridge, UK: Cambridge University Press, 1982. DOI: 10.1017/CBO9780511809477.

Kline, P., E. Rose, and C. Walters. "Systemic Discrimination Among Large U.S. Employers." Working paper, 2021.

Kline, Patrick M., Evan K. Rose, and Christopher R. Walters. *Systematic Discrimination Among Large U.S. Employers.* Cambridge, MA: National Bureau of Economic Research, 2021.

Leary, M. R. "Emotional responses to interpersonal rejection." *Dialogues Clinical Neuroscience* 17, no. 4 (2015): 435–41. DOI: 10.31887/DCNS.2015.17.4/mleary.

Park, Daeun, et al. "The development of grit and growth mindset during adolescence." *Journal of Experimental Child Psychology* 198 (2020): 104889. DOI: 10.1016/j.jecp.2020.104889.

Pfeffer, F. T., and A. Killewal. "Generations of Advantage. Multigenerational Correlations in Family Wealth." *Social Forces* 94, no. 4 (2018): 1411–42. DOI: 10.1093/sf/sox086.

Procter, Ian, and Maureen Padfield. "The Effect of the Interview on the Interviewee." *International Journal of Social Research Methodology* 1 (1998): 123–36. DOI: 10.1080/13645579.1998.10846868.

Randall, Ken, Mart Isaacson, and Carrie Ciro. "Validity and Reliability of the Myers-Briggs Personality Type Indicator: A Systematic Review and Meta-Analysis." *Journal of Best Practices in Health Professions Diversity* 10, no.1 (2017): 1–27. https://www.jstor.org/stable/26554264.

Rivera, Lauren A. "Hiring as Cultural Matching: The Case of Elite Professional Service Firms." *American Sociological Review* 77, no.6 (2012): 999–1022. DOI: 10.1177/0003122412463213.

Roberts, B. W., N. R. Kuncel, R. Shiner, et al. "The Power of Personality: The Comparative Validity of Personality Traits, Socioeconomic status, and Cognitive Ability for Predicting Important Life Outcomes." *Perspectives on Psychological Science* 2 (2007): 313–45. DOI: 10.1111/j.1745–6916.2007.00047.x.

Sheese, Brad E., and William G. Graziano. "Agreeableness." *Encyclopedia of Applied Psychology* (2004): 117–21. https://doi.org/10.1016/B0-12-657410-3/00020-9.

Smith, R. C., A. M. Dorsey, J. S. Lyles, and R. M. Frankel. "Teaching self-awareness enhances learning about patient-centered interviewing." *Academic Medicine* 74, no. 11 (1999): 1242–48, DOI: 10.1097/00001888-199911000-00020.

Srivastava, Sanjay, Oliver P. John, Samuel D. Gosling, and Jeff Potter. "Development of Personality in Early and Middle Adulthood: Set Like Plaster or Persistent Change?" *Journal of Personality and Social Psychology* 84, no. 5 (2003): 1041–53. DOI: 10.1037/0022-3514.84.5.1041.

Suleman, Q., M. A. Syed, Z. Mahmood, and I. Hussain. "Correlating Emotional Intelligence with Job Satisfaction: Evidence from a Cross-Sectional Study Among Secondary School Heads in Khyber Pakhtunkhwa, Pakistan." *Frontiers in Psychology* 11 (2020): 240. DOI: 10.3389/fpsyg.2020.00240.

Sutton, A. "Measuring the Effects of Self-Awareness: Construction of the Self-Awareness Outcomes Questionnaire." *European Journal of Psychology* 12, no. 4 (2016): 645–58. DOI: 10.5964/ejop.v12i4.1178.

Sutton, A., H. M. Williams, and C. W. Allinson. "A Longitudinal, Mixed Method Evaluation of Self-Awareness Training in the Workplace." *European Journal of Training and Development* 39, no. 7 (2015): 610–27, DOI: 10.1108/EJTD-04-2015-0031.

Tang, Christian Byrge. "Ethnic Heterogeneous Teams Outperform Homogeneous Teams on Well-defined but Not Ill-defined Creative Task." *Journal of Creativity and Business Innovation*, 2016: 2. http://www.journalcbi.com/ethnic-heterogeneous-teams-and -creativity.html.

Tuovinen S., X. Tang, and K. Salmela-Aro. "Introversion and Social Engagement: Scale Validation, Their Interaction, and Positive Association with Self-Esteem." *Frontiers in Psychology* 11 (2020): 590748. DOI: 10.3389/fpsyg.2020.590748.

Turner, Margery Austin, Peter Edelman, Erika Poethig, and Laudan Aron. *Tackling Persistent Poverty in Distressed Neighborhoods: History, Principles, and Strategies for Philanthropic Investment.* Washington, DC: Urban Institute, 2014.

United States Bureau of Labor Statistics. "Employer Costs for Employee Compensation Summary." Economic New Release, U.S. Dept. of Labor (March 17, 2023). https://www .bls.gov/news.release/ecec.nr0.htm.

United States Bureau of Labor Statistics. "Job Openings and Labor Turnover Survey." JOLTS, U.S. Dept. of Labor (March 8, 2023). https://www.bls.gov/jlt/home.htm.

Whalen, J.R., host. "There are More Open Jobs Than Ever Before. Why are Job Hunts Longer?" *Your Money Briefing. The Wall Street Journal* (January 23, 2023). https://www .wsj.com/podcasts/your-money-matters/there-are-more-open-jobs-than-ever- before-why-are-job-hunts-longer/184d00f8–8b3c-49af-887f-c543d67bc57e.

Xiang, Ping, and Amelia Lee. "Achievement Goals, Perceived Motivational Climate, and Students' Self-Reported Mastery Behaviors." *Research Quarterly for Exercise and Sport* 73, no. 1 (2002): 58–65. DOI: 10.1080/02701367.2002.10608992.

Zippia. "40 Important Job Interview Statistics [2023]: What You Need to Know Before Starting Your Job Search." Zippia.com. October 25, 2022. https://www.zippia.com /advice/job-interview-statistics/.

Index

About the Author

Anna Papalia is the CEO of Interviewology, a keynote speaker, and a career influencer with over 1.5 million followers across social media platforms. As a former director of talent acquisition turned career coach, she has advised more than ten thousand clients. Nominated for HR Person of the Year in 2020, she is a highly sought-after thought leader on all things interviewing.

Want to Discover Your Interview Style?

Start by taking the Interview Style Assessment
at www.TheInterviewology.com.

For more interview tips and additional resources,
follow Anna at:

anna..papalia   Anna Papalia   annapapalia   careercoachannapapalia